Barbara A

Quilts of Many Colors

Barbara Ann Smith

Barbara Ann Smith

Copyright © 2023 Barbara Ann Smith

All rights reserved.

Barbara Ann Smith

DEDICATION

This book is dedicated to the ones who encouraged me to try whatever I wanted; who nurtured my curiosity, faith, and courage; who taught me patience and perseverance until those projects were finished; and taught me never to give up on my dreams.

So, with great reverence, I honor my sweet mother, Maria; my brilliant brother, John; my dad, Al, who taught me the importance of self-discipline; and my third husband, Vaughn Bushman, who supported my writing. I also would like to thank husband number one, Calvin Lowell Smith, who taught me that a thing done by oneself is well cherished.

In addition, I would like to thank my grandmothers, Ninfa and Laura, and Aunt Julia, Aunt Jill, and Aunt Josie for their example to stand tough and never give up. I would also like to thank my brilliant and colorful friends Lu and Seymore Edmund Martinson, the former Assistant Attorney General of New York State under Nelson Rockefeller. He was the one who introduced me to the fine arts of Manhattan, Broadway shows, New York politics, and, oh yes, the latest dance steps.

A special tribute to all the people who inspired me to succeed: Armond Deschamps, Betty Beidelschies, Carol Finkel, Carole LaBue Brunstad, Melissa Blackington, Barbara Glantz, Helen Mullins, Joyce Lillicotch, Jacque Stafford, Orval L. Krieger of 37 Lamont Dr., Mike Kline, Patti Barrett, Calvin Lowell Smith, Mary Montgomery, and Deb and Terrance Haley and Ann Yeck.

And a very special word of thanks to all my brilliant and encouraging writing professors from Stanford University. *Bravo!*

Barbara Ann Smith

ACKNOWLEDGMENT

Behind every book is a team of people who put forth exemplary effort. *The Quilt of Many Colors* was crafted with the help of many talented individuals who assisted with my research.

I am thankful to Sandra Krieger, Ron Edwards, Beto Ferniza, his daughter Theresa and her husband Brent Holmes, Joyce Ramsey, and Dennis Hufford.

Moreover, I am grateful to my brilliant team at AMZ Book Publishers, without whose efforts this book would never have been published, refined, or distributed.

Last but not least, I wish to express my gratitude to my excellent editing team. The first is my talented friend Barbara Compton, who examined my manuscript with her investigative prowess and engendered spirit and helped me with some significant constructive criticism. She also helped design my book cover with a quilt her grandmother Mitty Stevens Bradshaw made in the late nineteenth century.

Next is Darlene Gsell, whose grammatical training is outstanding. Her corrections were invaluable in the first chapter.

Deb Haley, Doug Neilsen, Patti Barrett, and Cyd Rattunde offered many encouraging insights that helped clarify the story.

Barbara Ann Smith

CONTENTS

CHAPTER 1 KATRYN 1
   NEW YORK CITY, 1860 1
   TEN YEARS LATER 7
   ALL ABOARD 8

CHAPTER 2 MISS HAWTHORNE'S ACADEMY 11

CHAPTER 3 THE DURKHEIM DAIRY FARM 20
   SATURDAY MORNING AT 5:00 27

CHAPTER 4 THE HAUNTING MORMON PROPHECY 33
   TWO YEARS LATER 33

CHAPTER 5 THOMAS 42
   LIFE ON THE RANCH 44

CHAPTER 6 UTAH TERRITORY 51
   THE CHRISTMAS BALL 55

CHAPTER 7 THE RECOVERY / LEG OF LAMB 57
   LEG OF LAMB 59
   MEETING THOMAS'S PARENTS 62
   SIX O'CLOCK THE NEXT MORNING 66

CHAPTER 8 THE WEDDING OF THE CENTURY 68

CHAPTER 9 THE BIG NIGHT 72

CHAPTER 10 THE HONEYMOON 74
   GAMBLING SCENE ON THE TRAIN 76
   IN THE OXFORD CAR PLAYING CARDS 79

CHAPTER 11 THE PALACE HOTEL 81
   THE ENCOUNTER 85
   THE LUNCHEON 92

- CHAPTER 12 TRAIN TO UTAH TERRITORY 96
- CHAPTER 13 THE MORMON WAY 103
- CHAPTER 14 THE TWENTIETH ANNIVERSARY OF THE MOUNTAIN MEADOWS MASSACRE 109
- CHAPTER 15 THE WOMEN'S RELIEF SOCIETY 113
- CHAPTER 16 KATRYN'S MELTDOWN 120
  - Dear Mother and Father, ... 120
- CHAPTER 17 A TRIP BACK TO NEW YORK 126
- CHAPTER 18 THE GREAT WOMEN'S DEBATE OF APRIL 1875 134
  - The Debate Rules 134
- CHAPTER 19 HUNTING FOR ELK 148
- CHAPTER 20 GIDDY MADSEN AND THE FREEDOM TRIAL 155
  - Early 1850 155
- CHAPTER 21 THE UNDERGROUND MORMON RAILROAD 161
- CHAPTER 22 THE TRAIN LEAVES AT MIDNIGHT 166
  - Earlier That Evening 166
  - Brigham's Office the Next Morning 168
  - Back on the Train 169
- CHAPTER 23 WRANGLERS AND RUSTLERS ON THE ARIZONA STRIP 171
- CHAPTER 24 TWO LETTERS 175
  - My Dearest Katryn, ... 175
  - A Letter from Katryn 178
- CHAPTER 25 A NEAR-DEATH EXPERIENCE 179
- GLOSSARY OF MORMON TERMS 187
- NOTES 190
- SUGGESTED READING 191

Barbara Ann Smith

CHAPTER 1
KATRYN

Back in the mid and late nineteenth century, I walked a dangerous tightrope to exist in the world of my mother's secret past—one that was of brothels, champagne parties, sexual liaisons, and abortions. Was I a prostitute? Hell no! Was I a bastard? No again. The big question was this: How did I become Lady Katryn and then become a Mormon wife two thousand miles from New York City, where I was born?

New York City, 1860

In a mystical land over thirty-six hundred miles from Paris, one can find a city of three hundred thirty-eight thousand immigrants hungering to fulfill their dreams of success. They dreamed of building a better and more prosperous life for themselves and their families, speaking freely, and living where they could practice the religion of their choice or practice no religion at all. In essence, New York was an emporium of immigrants where wishing and dreaming were infectious and where wealth wasn't just for the elite but was attainable for all who dared to take risks, work hard, and harbor a relentless American spirit to persevere until they achieved their goals.

New York City was an ambitious hustle-and-bustle town in 1860 with red-and-white-striped hot dog stands on corners with lots of dripping yellow mustard and mouth-watering sauerkraut. The hot dogs sold for three cents apiece or two for five cents. Elegant horse-drawn carriages transported the Sacred Four Hundred—New York's upper classes—to church, lunch, and parties; sloops and sailboats cruised on the Hudson River with the idle rich aboard; children played ball in Central Park with their nannies. The merchants reached clients upriver by transporting their goods on Fulton's steamboat. Moreover, the women smiled and proudly walked tall with shoulders back and heads held high, having obtained their right to own property, sue in their name, and handle their business affairs. Everyone was going about their business like the sun would never set or the good times would never end as they effused an attitude of indifference to anything happening outside the prosperous and trendy city of New York, a magical land where dreams do come true.

Furthermore, 1860 was strategically a significant year for some. It was twelve months before the first large battle of the Civil War at Bull Run, Virginia—and believe me, New York's inhabitants started paying attention to life outside their magnificent community of culture and wealth. This happened after a group of Confederate soldiers fired fatal shots at the Union troops at Fort Sumter, South Carolina, which started the Civil War on April 12, 1861, and bloody well lasted until the spring of 1881.

Also, in 1860, women were starting to come of age and become more assertive in running their affairs. Some women ventured out of their comfort zone and owned mercantile businesses, like clothing factories, millinery shops, and greenhouses. The more intellectual young women went to college to teach; some even embraced the law and medical professions. Some brave souls were even compelled to nurse the wounded soldiers after the Civil War ended.

In contrast, out in the Wild West, in a wilderness called Utah Territory, some New York women gave birth to Mormon babies, shot Blackhawks, and tended to their gardens as their only source of fruits and vegetables. They sew clothes at home on a foot-pedal Singer sewing machine, which was lucky to have made it on the treacherous trek westward in a Conestoga wagon. If these women didn't have one, they mended and made clothes by hand or ordered shirts, dresses, and hats from the Montgomery Ward catalog if they were rich.

Getting a college education in the early history of the Latter-day Saints was unheard of and not encouraged for Mormon women. Vocational training was espoused by Brigham Young, who saw the need for only male apprentices, journeymen, and master artisans. The need for academic scholars came later. At this point, it would be fair to mention that Brigham Young came from a rural background in Vermont, where education was lacking; thus, he was illiterate most of his life. How he was able to read the Book of Mormon is still a mystery. Perhaps his favorite wife, Amelia, read him a verse daily?

Back in New York City in 1860, a very different type of woman evolved: the entrepreneurial business executive called the madam, who owned brothels and managed a harem of beautiful, lusty women. Lower Manhattan was infested with over three thousand prostitutes pleasuring their johns 24-7. During the summers, more women plied their trade, coming from nearby towns and the state of New Jersey, which would drive the population of hookers up to ten thousand. Some husbands, desperate to put food on the table and pay rent, even encouraged their wives just to perform fellatio for extra money. The wives would rent a room just for the season and then return home with plenty of money to keep their family in brisket, beer, milk, and clothes for the rest of the year. The Irish and Italians had at least, on average, six to nine children to raise. But the Italian women were loaned out to no one. Their husbands were very proud and religious—not that the Irish weren't—and occasionally, when their wives were pregnant, they would visit a brothel for sexual healing. For them, it was all about keeping their wives' lips pure to kiss their angelic children.

At this point, I would like to mention that Katryn's mother had only been with one man before she met the Duke, which was unusual behavior for a prostitute since promiscuity, not monogamy, was the norm in the brothels of New York.

The hookers, on the other hand, followed a strict code of ethics. Stealing another woman's john, clothes, or makeup was taboo. Lipstick was always scented—that was how wives knew what their husbands were up to. It was like the women were sending a message home—"We are taking good care of yours truly while you have your baby or frigid moment." It was an unwritten pact between women of the night and married women of a moral nature. And, of course, the men were totally unaware this code existed.

Also, it was interesting to discover what prostitutes carried in their purses. Julie carried a fork to heighten her johns' senses during ejaculations; meanwhile, Sally had lemons with the pulp scooped out hidden in her vagina to prevent unwanted pregnancies. Darla carried a little piggy bank to keep her cash close during tricks, and Frenchie carried watered-down perfume to rinse off her john's manhood and clean out her mouth. Each young woman carried a small white pearl-trimmed handgun and a small knife for protection from sadistic men who got pleasure out of torturing them—and a washcloth soaked with strong bourbon to kill germs.

The infamous prostitutes of New York City during the nineteenth century worked out of brothels, hotels, boardinghouses, theaters, alleyways, street corners, and fancy carriages.

An interesting fact about the brothels is that each of these "emporiums of pleasure" carried its brand of distinction. Fannie's boasted silk sheets and pillowcases donned with white fluffy down comforters, and paying johns were treated to a breakfast of champions—chocolate candies served with creamed tea and crumpets.

Stevens's served cold beer, bratwurst, sauerkraut, and pretzels between tricks to their johns.

Zachary gave Swedish massages to gay couples seeking a hideaway to relax and enjoy the forbidden.

The Golden Circus had an all-naked female review standing in lesbian poses that changed every three minutes.

The Red Rose gave out complimentary feathered fans to help with tickling scrotums.

Kate Wood's Hotel de Wood was lavishly furnished with expensive clocks and furniture and over $10,000 worth of famous oil paintings from the Renaissance period.

Frenchie's gave out the obvious to each patron after he made fifteen paid visits. There was never a cover charge, but after visiting a brothel, a man would spend extra money on red roses, red velvet heart-shaped boxes of chocolate-covered candy cherries, and silver trinkets for his remarkable delectable woman. All of these could be bought at each emporium of pleasure for ten dollars.

Women of pleasure were passionately appreciated and loved by the johns. Wives could never compete with these amorously experienced women who came with a bag of exotic tricks that made men scream with endless joy. Our heroine, Katryn Kline Wellington, would later share these treasured secrets to save many Mormon marriages.

"Fleur-de-lis"—whatever one desires—was the prostitute's motto. Occasionally, New York police officers would escort the johns to their women for discretion and a fee of five dollars. These johns came from all walks of life: sailors, waterfront dockworkers, desperate husbands, clergy members, gays, people in business, politicians, and foreigners. The list of patrons was endless and growing daily, just like the prostitutes' income.

The women of the night made $100,000 to $300,000 a year in today's currency. They became rich and invested the money wisely, such as in real estate, church pews, cotton commodities, stocks, or government bonds. Some prostitutes even started their own brothels. Women were perceived as dumb and desperate and in need of a man to survive in the late nineteenth century, but actually, these women were street-smart. During their pillow talk, they learned a great deal from their wealthy johns and put this information to good use when negotiating their business deals.

"God is great, God is good, God loves free-spirited women!" sang Katryn Kline, or Princess as she was known around the New York City Bowery in the 1860s. She was slim, five feet, six inches tall, with colossal, creamy, well-developed breasts. Her curly hair was a reddish blonde, with piercing baby-blue eyes peeking from under her wispy bangs. Her personality matched her looks: warm, friendly, and vivacious. But her untouched fresh womanhood—perceived as perfectly intact and tight as a baby's fist—drove men to propose three or four times a week. Sad to say, for her admirers, Princess was fifteen and a gorgeous virgin, and none of the women held that little tidbit against her. They loved the way she always treated them with respect and the skillful way she fixed their ripped sexy lingerie.

Katryn also assisted with many early abortions with the infamous Ann Loman of the Tenderloin District in Lower Manhattan, saving many of the women's careers and, in some instances, their lives. Abortions in those days consisted of taking powders or pills to end the pregnancy immediately or using a surgical instrument for late terminations. Katryn abhorred the latter unless it was to save the mother's life. Furthermore, a late-term abortion could be substituted for adoption if the fetus lived after delivery. But there were so many hungry and homeless children needing homes that sometimes this option was not chosen.

Nevertheless, Ann Loman and her pretty young assistant tried to adopt out as many babies as possible to loving parents and a good home, one where there was plenty of food to eat, clean clothes to wear, and spiritual teachings to save the soul. Food for thought: one of Joseph Smith's best friends was Dr. John C. Bennett, an abortionist. A fascinating fact is that Joseph Smith had forty-four wives but only had children with his first wife, Emma. It is time to think outside the box!

Lady Katryn was born of a Jewish prostitute, Frenchie, and an English Austrian aristocrat, Duke, with ties to Queen Victoria of England and the House of Hapsburg in Austria. He sure loved to take Frenchie to the opera on Broadway for a night of pure pleasure of the flesh while listening to Mozart's *The Magic Flute*. Those violins really helped his erotic senses explode in those dark balconies on the upper third floor. A little bit of voyeurism was an added high for this lusty couple.

Katryn's maternal grandparents, Isaac and Emma Kline, were of good German and Austrian stock. They had owned a Swiss dairy. After the taxes on their property went sky-high, they sold the farm and bought tickets for a Paris steamer headed for New York. Their delicate Anna Marie (Frenchie) was only fifteen and was promised to her uncle in marriage when she turned sixteen. But she refused to marry him and ran off to the Bowery, where her beauty, youth, and French accent earned her the company of John Jacob Astor III, one of the wealthiest men in New York City. He was an American financier and philanthropist and had served as a brave soldier in the

American Civil War. Smitten by her charms, he lavished her with jewels and fancy furs.

One evening John was ill with a spring cold, so he sent his most trusted friend, the Third Duke of Wellington, to give Frenchie money so she wouldn't need to service other men. But it was lust at first sight once the duke and the duchess met. They quickly headed for the theater on Broadway. After climbing three flights of plush red-carpeted stairs, they got to work. Later they learned they had conceived a baby-blue-eyed daughter on the fainting couch on that fateful April night in 1850.

Nine months later, Katryn was born with rosy-pink cheeks, piercing blue eyes, a tiny aristocratic chiseled nose, and light blonde hair with red highlights—an Austrian princess, if there ever was one. She was beautiful and delicate, always smiling for her daddy, who Queen Victoria had called to visit India to help keep the peace between the Sikhs and the Hindus, a post he held for ten years. But he always slipped money inside his romantic letters to Frenchie to raise little Katryn and send her to the best finishing school in Lancaster, Pennsylvania, Miss Hawthorne's, where her destiny would be altered forever.

Ten Years Later

"Darling daughter," Frenchie said, "are you ready to catch the train for Lancaster? If we don't hurry, we will miss it and must wait three more days, which will mean missing orientation, which is so important in a new school. Don't you think, dear?"

"Mother, I don't understand why you can't trust me to make this trip alone. I am all grown up, and I get that curse every month like clockwork. Doesn't the curse mean I can get married and have children, which must equate to being a mature woman who can travel alone?"

"Never mind that now, dear. Just hurry. We will discuss your womanhood on the train," replied Frenchie.

All Aboard

"Mother, this is a beautiful, luxurious railroad car to ride in. I love the gold and silver wallpaper made from fine New York linen, and the Austrian chandeliers are so sparkly and colorful that when the sun hits their crystals, a prism bursts with red, blue, and yellow hues. Also, the magnificent Chinese red lotus blossoms are huge—like Easter lilies. I love them!" exclaimed Katryn. "Is the food as good as this place looks, Mother?"

"Nothing but the best for you, Princess," her mother replied. "Dad's best friend, Mr. Vanderbilt, owns it, and he has one on most lines. And they all look identical with kelly-green velvet curtains, gold fringe, and matching ties. Underneath these velvets are very sheer white Irish lace curtains delicately made with heavenly white wispy embroidered circles going up and down."

"Mother, the curtains are elegant, but I am famished. Isn't it time for lunch? May we dine in the club car, where they have white linen tablecloths and Waterford crystal stem glasses? I also heard that an Austrian violinist plays Mozart during tea at 4:00 p.m. And the skilled Irish immigrant waiters serve English breakfast tea on a sterling silver tea tray with a vase of pink roses and cherry almond scones placed on dainty white dishes hand-painted with pink rosebuds and accompanied by white lacy tea napkins. You will love it, Mother," Katryn said.

Frenchie just smiled as she winked at her intelligent, enchanting blue-eyed daughter. "My dear, you are well versed on table etiquette and menus for this train. I'm impressed," she exclaimed. "Where did you learn all this information? No, don't tell me; let me guess. From your father. But of course! Speaking of your father, here is a recent letter he sent you. But don't read it until after breakfast."

Over a sumptuous brunch of eggs Benedict, ham, freshly squeezed orange juice, succulent large red grapes, and jubilant English tea with sweet cream, mother, and daughter discussed orientation. Afterward, Katryn read her letter from the Duke of Wellington, her invisible father, for ten years.

My Darling Princess,

You are so precious to me, my little one. When I return home, life will be exciting. We will all go swimming and sailing on the Atlantic, enjoy picnics of deviled eggs, cucumber, and cream cheese sandwiches, drink strawberry lemonade from long-stemmed crystal glasses, and eat pheasant to our hearts' content. Oh, darling, I will make my long absence up to you. Please do your humble father a favor and surprise me with high grades so you can attend Saint Katherine's Nursing School before you settle down and marry. It was my sister Evelyn's dream to become a surgical nurse, but God took her to heaven with him instead. He must have had something more important up there for her to do. I chose Miss Hawthorne's Academy because there, girls learn how to think on their feet and make wise decisions besides learning the usual academics, home economics, and manners, which are all important for a well-rounded education. Bye, for now, my little princess. See you soon!

I love you very much,
Your devoted father

Katryn folded the letter as tears streamed down her rosy cheeks. "I miss and love you too, Father," she whispered as she kissed the letter, leaving a pink impression of her delicate lips, and put it in her purse.

"Mother, when is Father coming home to us?"

"Heaven only knows, darling. He has to stop in London to conclude some big business deal first."

"Well, I only have one more question, Mother. Does Mr. Vanderbilt have a car on the Orient Express that goes to India?"

"Katryn Kline Wellington, you are hilarious!" her mother proclaimed. "Let's give your father some time to answer my letter, which I sent two days ago to India. For now, make your father proud with high grades. And please stay in shape by playing fencing, tennis, dancing, or dressage. You know how your dear father loves his sports—field hockey and rugby, and you can enjoy them together as spectators when he returns."

Brunch was finished, and a nap was in order back in the Vanderbilt car. Time fluttered by as the walnut grandfather clock chimed four times—time for afternoon tea. The two Wellington females had to hurry before all those sweet delectable treats were gone.

God is great, God is good, and God loves New York!

CHAPTER 2
MISS HAWTHORNE'S ACADEMY

The train pulled into Pennsylvania Station at six o'clock sharp, two hours later. The school carriage was there to whisk Katryn and her mother away to Miss Hawthorne's Academy for orientation.

Better late than never! The two of them arrived at orientation ten minutes late, and oh, did they receive a great many raised eyebrows and frown lines from the professors and giggles from Katryn's classmates. Nevertheless, the two Wellingtons held their heads up very high on their shoulders like two gazelles, listening to every word the headmistress spoke. Then they heard silence and knew what would come next—a loud, piercing voice that hurt their ears:

"Ladies, to whom do I owe this rude display of manners creeping past my long Roman nose and crawling under the pew like a turtle with big blackjack bulging eyes?"

"The Wellingtons," the duchess whispered with a tremble of great fear. "We humbly apologize and promise never to be late again."

"Apology accepted!"

By the time Katryn and her mother found their room, they were exhausted with swollen red eyes and wispy disheveled hairdos—a sight to behold!

"Hello, I am Lizbeth Durkheim, your roommate. I am delighted to meet you. I can tell you both are tired, and it would take a long hour to ride the carriage to the Lancaster Hotel. Your mother is welcome to sleep on my bed."

"Thank you very much," Mrs. Wellington said. "You are so nice and helpful. I know you and my daughter will get along splendidly. She is a serious student like you and must do well to make her daddy proud. He is in India for a spell but keeps in touch by writing us once a month. Excuse me for sneezing. Where is the ladies' room?"

"Down the hall and to the right," replied Lizbeth. "It is a combination bath and toilet. There are plenty of towels, sponges, perfumed soaps, and body creams. Cleanliness is always encouraged here at Miss Hawthorne's, so make yourself at home. If you need anything, I will be next door. Alice has an extra bed until she gets another roommate; her last one ran off and got married."

The girls chuckled when they heard the hardwood floor squeak as Mrs. Wellington walked down the wide violet-colored, rosebud-wallpapered hallway, shaking her blondish-red curls and thinking that her daughter would never leave this outstanding school before graduation. Katryn had too much of her father in her to be a quitter. In addition, Katryn loved to read and write. Someday she would become a famous author like Emily Brontë or Mark Twain. She had read many of their books and wrote stories and poems in her journal daily. *I know she will stay here and become a great scholar,* her mother thought. *After all, she has always been a straight-A student.*

"So, how are the winters here in Pennsylvania?" Katryn asked with a childlike inquisitive smile.

"Very snowy, cold, and long. But you will never notice since we receive enormous amounts of homework. Every week we must read two books and give both a written and an oral report on Fridays. We don't sleep much at Miss Hawthorne's."

"What happens on Saturdays and Sundays?" Katryn asked with a puzzled look.

"Nothing! No one stays here on weekends. That's when the fun begins, but I'll tell you about it later," Lizbeth said. "Every morning, we are permitted to sleep until eight o'clock. Breakfast is at ten, tea is at four, and supper is at seven. And you'd better not be late, or you will just be given oatmeal. In between, we learn about social graces and crafts like embroidery, crochet, and a game called bridge. Music, such as the piano and the harp, is also taught. Do you love music, Katryn?"

"Yes, the piano is my passion. I can play Beethoven's Fifth and Mozart's Concerto in D Minor blindfolded. What about you?"

"The harp is my great love, and Mama says I play like an angel. Hey, we can practice together and perhaps perform at our annual school Christmas concert."

Katryn smiled and responded, "Absolutely, we will perform together. I welcome the challenge."

"Katryn, I have always wondered what New York City is like. Do tell," Lizbeth asked with a schoolgirl's curiosity.

"Are you ready for some shockers?" Katryn asked. Katryn didn't wait for Lizbeth to reply. She loved to describe her favorite city, where she had many girlfriends and male admirers and lived in a substantial orange brick Georgian colonial home with large white pillars on the front porch and a black slate roof. This home was considered one of Manhattan's most magnificent and well-constructed homes. The duke had commissioned the famous New York City architect John P. Gaynor to build it.

"I'm impressed; I shall visit you one day," Lizbeth said.

"Well, my hometown is made up of the following five boroughs: the Bronx, Brooklyn, Staten Island, Queens, and Manhattan. Manhattan is where I live, and I love what Manhattan has to offer regarding culture. We have the Astor Opera House, Broadway plays, musical concerts in Central Park, historical museums, and holiday parades. If you are so inclined, a woman can attend college to become a teacher or a nurse. Education is highly treasured in New York because it is the gateway to a new world of forbidden and exotic philosophies and a breeding ground for the intellectual. I always read the classics, and I enjoy poetry by Emily Brontë. My favorite poem by her is 'Come Hither, Child,' written in 1839," Katryn said.

"I must hear all about the opera, Katryn. Are the seats wrapped in red velvet? And did Caruso sing there? I love his baritone voice," Lizbeth exclaimed.

"Yes, and yes," Katryn answered. "But first, I must give you a little history of New York City. It started with a few thousand Indians who sold Manhattan to the Dutch in 1724 for twenty-four dollars' worth of trinkets. In 1749 the Dutch lost it to the British, who later surrendered it to the Americans in 1881. God is great. Also, Lizbeth, New York City has become a melting pot of cultures, with each nationality assimilating into one—American culture! Which makes good sense. We live in a brand-new world, and everyone here in America—except for the loyal English Tories—fought for freedom and liberty, which makes us brothers and sisters in the same cause, sort of like a religion," Katryn proudly said.

"I agree wholeheartedly!" Lizbeth yelled out. "Tell me more about the buildings, please! Are they all as big as your house, Katryn?"

"Well, some buildings are taller and bigger with many windows. The views are spectacular from some roofs. On a clear day, one can see the Statue of Liberty, which France gave us as a symbol of our freedom as a new country. The French fought alongside our rebels during the Revolutionary War and did a fantastic job of stopping the British from winning. I just love Paris in the springtime with all the irises, hyacinths, and lilacs blooming along the Seine River."

"You've been to Paris?" Lizbeth asked. "I have always wanted to go there. You are so lucky you are rich, Katryn. I'd never be able to afford to go anywhere, and I barely can pay to attend Miss Hawthorne's School. Fortunately, my dad pays my tuition with two hundred pounds of pork, one hundred dozen eggs, a variety of fruits and vegetables—apples, pears, cabbages, onions, and beets—and one hundred fifty gallons of milk from our dairy cows. And this is monthly," she added.

"Well, you don't have to worry about money now that you know me. I'm rich!" Katryn responded. "My father will help you in any way he can. He is always looking for fertile land, pigs, fine horses, and antiques to invest in," Katryn said. "Sounds like you have an overabundance of land and animals to me. What about antiques?"

"All kinds, sister! When you visit me, you will see everything we own. Maybe you can make a list, and I'll draw some pictures. Art is my passion, and I am good at it. Once, I was commissioned by our Baptist minister, Mr. Armstrong, to draw a Nativity scene for our Christmas pageant. Everyone loved it, and now it is hanging in our chapel," Lizbeth proudly said.

"I am impressed," Katryn exclaimed. "Can I tell you more about New York tomorrow? I am talked out," she said.

"Sure, I understand."

Mrs. Wellington returned and said, "Lights out, girls. I need to rise at six to catch the train back to New York."

And so life at Miss Hawthorne's began for Katryn Kline Wellington. Her class schedule was full. French, classical English and French literature were the most fascinating to Katryn. So was English riding and jumping over fences. The students never attended a hunt but were trained to do so in case the opportunity presented itself later in life when they were married to wealthy plantation owners in the mighty South. Dressage was taught, and the girls competed for first-, second-, and third-place ribbons, which were a big honor to win.

One evening in their bedroom, Lizbeth asked an obvious question of Katryn: "Now that you have one week under your belt, would you like to come home with me this weekend? In fact, you may spend every weekend with my family and me. It gets pretty lonely here at school after three o'clock on Fridays, and our bishop gives the most thought-provoking sermons on Sunday mornings."

"Aren't you the generous one, Lizbeth! Of course, I will join you. I am looking forward to meeting your wonderful family. What shall I bring to wear for a farm?"

Lizbeth chuckled, then responded with a list of clothing: "Boots, long stockings, a light jacket and warm sweater, a hat that ties under the chin, a long Sunday church dress, and clean underwear for three days."

"What about tennis clothes and a bathing suit?" asked Katryn.

Lizbeth frowned and puckered up her freshly wet lips, then shook her beautiful shiny brown hair back and forth.

"I get it," Katryn replied. "No tennis or swimming allowed. By the way, how are we traveling to your farm?"

"My parents will send one of my five brothers to pick us up," Lizbeth answered.

"Nice touch, a chauffeur! Will the carriage be an enclosed one like the Amish use?" Katryn asked. "You know my hair must be perfect. After all, it is imperative that I make a great impression on your parents, and they may not want me to be your roommate if my hair is unruly."

"My goodness, Miss Prissy, you sure are particular. Are all New Yorkers like you?" Lizbeth asked.

"Yes, ma'am! Money, breeding, and fashion are very important to us New Yorkers—and in that order," Katryn proudly exclaimed with a passionate voice. "For example, there is a certain way a woman wears her hair that tells her true moral character. Take, for instance, when I wear my hair pulled back in waves, cascading down my back; I am sending a message of flowering innocence that yearns to be plucked, but only after marriage. But if I color my hair red and puff it up all over my head with a beret and put red rouge on my cheeks and lips, I am sending a message that I am ready to be plucked—marriage is not needed, just fifty dollars."

"Katryn, my delicate ears are burning. You're kidding, right? I've never heard such vulgar language," Lizbeth said with a chuckle. "Please, no more. My ears can't take it."

"No, I am not kidding. I know you have animals on your farm that mate and have babies. And I bet my life you have watched the dirty deed and messy birth many times."

Lizabeth just held up her arms, cocked her head, and frowned with elevens in the middle of her forehead. Her face was bright red from embarrassment.

"Roomie, I know I am going to learn more about life from you than here at Miss Hawthorne's."

Friday came, and Lizbeth's brother Timothy pulled up outside Miss Hawthorne's. On his head, he wore a straw hat with a black ribbon band over his bushy red hair, which was popping out all over. Both Lizbeth and Katryn looked at his hair, puffing out from the sides of his hat. Then they looked at each other and burst into uncontrollable laughter, making their faces red, and their eyes shed comedic tears.

"What's up with you ladies? If it's a joke, I want to hear it," Timothy exclaimed. Then he started to laugh at how silly their faces looked. So Lizbeth told him about New Yorkers, according to Katryn. He began to laugh, but not as uncontrollably as his sister and her friend.

"So, little sister, please introduce me to this beautiful creature."

"Brother Timothy, may I present my new friend and roommate, Miss Katryn Kline Wellington, from New York City."

"Very pleased to make your acquaintance. Any friend of my sister is a friend of mine for life," Timothy said as he winked at Katryn, who nodded back.

Oh dear, Katryn thought, another admirer whom I do not care to fraternize with. He shows some good breeding, but that red hair, just like Mother's—unruly and bright red with blond highlights, and lots of it. It needs the correct shampoo and conditioner. Oh well, not my problem. Spoken like a true New Yorker. *I have enough on my plate trying to make a good impression on Lizbeth's parents. The minute I arrive, I will freshen up by brushing my hair so* it will shine, and then I'll dust off my clothes. The roads here are all black dirt—dusty and muddy. I wouldn't ride a mule through these thick mud puddles. So unladylike!

Timothy stretched his back, then sat straight up to improve his posture. He took a deep breath.

"Katryn, would you like to see his prized sorrel horses?"

"Of course, I would; horses are my favorite animal," she responded. "I have been riding since I was three, and my father insisted I learn dressage early."

"Dre ... what?" Timothy asked.

"Dressage is an exquisite team effort by the rider and horse. It is also the highest expression of horse training, where the horse and rider perform a series of predetermined movements from memory. I have won three blue ribbons at London's annual international dressage event. Tomorrow I will show you how it is done."

"Where and when?"
Katryn asked, "Do you have a very obedient horse, Timothy?"

"Yes! Meet me at the barn tomorrow at sunrise," he replied. "Wait till you see our magnificent horses. You'll love their rich sorrel color with honey-colored manes and tails that stand straight up when they gallop."

"They sound glorious to ride. Oh, Lizbeth, are you joining us? I simply will not go without a chaperone. So, you see, your presence is imperative!"

Lizbeth just rolled her eyes and nodded her head, making her gold-tinted ponytail swish.

"I take that as a yes," Katryn said.

The elegant black and yellow landau carriage pulled by two well-muscled chestnut-colored Morgan horses drove off into the pink coral sunset toward the Durkheim farm and dairy.

CHAPTER 3
THE DURKHEIM DAIRY FARM

It was 5:00 p.m. when Timothy drove the carriage around the front of the big burnt-orange brick house where Lizbeth's parents lived with her five siblings: perky Joshua, bashful Timothy, pigtailed Karen, and little Mary, and wild Zack—fourteen, twenty, twelve, and seven-year-old fraternal twins, respectively. Big brother jumped out of the carriage to assist the young women onto the wraparound Victorian porch with freshly painted white turrets.

"I'll see you two inside. And, Katryn, please save me a seat next to you at the dinner table, preferably on your left side. I have something I want to whisper in your ear," Timothy said.

"Okay," Katryn answered.

The girls held their fits of laughter until they went into the foyer. Then they let out continual comedic sidesplitting laughter that turned their faces red.

"What's all this schoolgirl humor about?" Papa asked.

He was the first person they met when they walked into the house; he was lighting the candles in the hallway since it was almost dark outside. Lizbeth and Katryn continued to laugh, even louder now until they walked into the kitchen and smelled the pot roast cooking on top of the stove. Katryn could always smell a pork roast when sauerkraut accompanied it.

Lizbeth couldn't help but ask when it would be ready. It smelled delicious, with garlic and onions. She loved to pile the kraut on top of her mashed potatoes and slowly chew one soft, crunchy bite at a time.

"Ten minutes, ladies. Please wash your hands in the kitchen sink, then help me set the table. Everything, including the tablecloth, is over on the sideboard, and I took everything out last evening for your homecoming dinner," Mother said.

Mother smiled at the new guest and pointed to Lizbeth to show her where Katryn should sit.

"I presume you are my daughter's roommate from New York City with a name?" she asked. "You may call me Mama."

Lizbeth butted in, "Please forgive my country manners, Mother. May I present my friend and roommate, princess Katherine Kline Wellington from New York City. Her dad's a real duke from England with royal ties to Austrian royalty, the Hapsburgs ruled the Holy Roman Empire for over six hundred forty years, and her great-aunt was Marie Antoinette, who was beheaded."

"What about your mother, Katryn? Where are her people from?"

"My mother is from very wealthy merchants who go back to Jesus's time."

"I see," Lizbeth's mother said with frown lines on her forehead. "Finish setting the table with Grandmother's Waterford crystal stemware, please. I made mint iced tea with sugar, lemon, and a seven-layer white coconut cake. Usually, I make the proverbial German chocolate cake, but I decided to dress it up for this special occasion of meeting you, Katryn."

"Oh, you have made me feel very welcome. Thank you, Mrs. Durkheim—I mean Mama."

Before long, everyone was seated at the table, including Timothy, who sat on the left side of Katryn.

Papa asked Timothy to say grace so he could show off his spiritual side to the new guest. But first, he introduced her to the rest of the family.

"Heavenly Father, thank you for all the blessings you have given my family this harvest. We will share our bounty with the poor, widows, and our church. Please keep us holy and righteous so we can all minister to our neighbors, help our country thrive, and govern the states just and humbly. In the name of Jehovah, amen!"

"That was the most beautiful prayer I have ever heard, Timothy. Thank you for sharing," Katryn said.

"I agree," Papa said.
"Me too." Mama nodded.
"Well, I guess it was okay," Lizbeth remarked.
Timothy was overjoyed and embarrassed; his face was as red as a garden beet.
"So, how do you like Miss Hawthorne's?" Mama asked Katryn.

"She likes it just fine, Mama. Please let her eat. Then we can all go inside the parlor after dinner, where Katryn will tell us all about New York City."

"That's perfect for me," Mama said. "I will bring some triple chocolate chip oatmeal cookies to crunch on while we all listen."

Everyone hurried through dinner so they could eat Mama's prize blue-ribbon cookies and learn about New York City.

In the parlor, Lizbeth was setting up two butcher paper canvases for Katryn, indicating that she should draw a map of New York City on one and list pertinent information on the other.

"Everyone, before I commence drawing the map, I think it best to tell a little history of Manhattan, where I live.

"Once upon a time, on a big parcel of land, inhabitants known as the Lenape Indians roamed New York. Then one day, a group of explorers landed in what we know today as upstate New York; they were the mighty Dutch who ruled the great oceans and fought and won many wars in the fifteenth century. The Dutch originally sailed to the shores of New France, Canada, where Quebec is today. They migrated down Lake Erie to the Hudson River valley and discovered Manhattan. It was love and greed at first sight. The Dutch knew a good opportunity when they encountered this magical island of beautiful cedar trees; enchanted flowers with opulent fragrances of lavender, wild rose, mountain laurel, and flowering dogwood; bountiful wild game birds like wild turkey and Canada honkers; and white-tailed deer and pheasants fluttering and strolling around the countryside of green hills and deep, lush meadows. Someone anonymous once said that Manhattan is like heaven where angels abound, leading us to great riches and adventures," Katryn described.

Katryn asked everyone if they could guess the price the Dutch had paid for beautiful Manhattan. Joshua raised his hand and said he had learned in school it was twenty-four Dutch guilders, but it came in the form of wampum and colorful trinkets.

"Correct, Joshua. The Indians proudly wore these items while dancing beside a warm fire surrounded by large sparkly granite rocks with elm wood in the center. Good job! Some wampum and trinkets," Katryn continued explaining, "were hung in lodges where the sun's rays could slip through the door openings and shine through the trinkets, which elicited red, orange, yellow, green, blue, and violet hues.

"Does anyone want to venture a guess as to why this happens?" No one answered, so Katryn explained.

"It's because some of the trinkets were crystal triangular prisms where a single white light can be separated into its component colors, like I just mentioned. I'll tell you what, I will bring a prism from our science class next weekend, and we will experiment and write a little description about what it looks like hanging in your kitchen window," Katryn promised.

Everyone clapped and cheered, especially the younger children.

"Okay, students, let's continue with the map," said the girl from New York. "All eyes up here. I have drawn Manhattan first with the three bodies of water that surround it: the Hudson River to the west, the East River, and the Harlem River that separates the Bronx from Manhattan, making it an island. And to the southeast of all these rivers is the Atlantic Ocean, which they eventually empty into. One tidbit that is important to remember about the land under Manhattan is that many large granite deposits settled there from the beginning of time; this deposit would prove invaluable when building tall churches. These rocks provided the strong foundation needed to support all the stones the churches are made from. Such as the Second Reformed Dutch Church on Arthur Kill Road, built in 1808; the Quaker Meeting House, built in 1818; the Second Free African Church of St. Philip, built in 1822; the Second Free Presbyterian Church, built in 1832; the Friends Meeting House that was converted into a Jewish synagogue—Ansche Chesed—built in 1840; the Episcopal St. John's Chapel, built in 1803; the Broadway Tabernacle, built in 1836; the Church of the Messiah, built in 1839; St. George's Church, built in 1840; St. Ann's Church, built in 1840; Hanson Place Central Methodist Church, built in 1847; Madison Square Presbyterian Church, built in 1853; the German Evangelical Church, built in 1857; and the Church of St. Gabriel, built in 1859."

"Boy, that was a lot of churches, Miss Katryn," Timothy said. "Why were there so many?"

"That's an excellent question. Does anyone want to venture a guess?"

"Because of good old-fashioned hardworking immigrants like me; my father, Karl; and my grandfather Helmick. They came from the Old Country of Bavaria, which is part of Germany. They helped build several churches before they migrated to Pennsylvania," Papa said with a proud heart. "Isn't that so, Mama?"

Mama just nodded affirmatively, as always when her husband commanded it so. *Just two peas in a pod!* Lizbeth thought.

"Yes, Papa and Mama Durkheim, those are good answers. There were many immigrants—the Dutch, the Scots, freed blacks, enslaved African Americans, indentured servants, the English, the French, the Jewish, the Irish, the Germans, the Greeks, the Swiss, the Austrians, the Polish, the Italians, and the Chinese, and many more from many countries, who pooled their culture and skills to make their experiences in their New World a success. They shared things with and helped their neighbors until they were one big assimilated geographic family, especially after the French and Indian War. Moreover, the Revolutionary War had occupied so much of their time, money, and hard labor, plus fighting in the wars to protect their new homeland. They were a group to be proud of. They're the foundation our country was built upon, like a quilt of many colors.

"Now, by the 1800s," Katryn continued, "New York City was the most popular and successful seaport in the world. Everybody who traded for a living wanted to bring their goods to America because, after the wars, it was ripe for luxury. We enjoyed exporting our fine linen from New York and Pennsylvania; our adopted corn, Southern cotton, and country-pure beef to England, France, Germany, and Italy; and our Kentucky bourbon and wines to the West Indies and beyond."

"Are there farms in Manhattan? And how do big-city people get around? Do they eat the same foods as country people?" little Mary asked, almost out of breath.

"Wow, three great questions, Mary," remarked Katryn. "Let's see if I can answer them by telling you a secret. City people eat the same food as country folks: butter, white or dark rye bread, sugar cookies, chocolate cakes, homemade vanilla ice cream, fish, beef, chicken, and mutton. Only the rich can eat out in expensive restaurants or have their food bought by their chefs and prepared in their own kitchens. Some of the city people use a community garden or their own backyard to grow delicious healthy vegetables and many fruit trees such as apples, cherries, apricot, and peach. Some city slickers have room for chickens and a milk cow in their yards. And, of course, there are big farms on the outskirts of Manhattan. What do you think of those answers, Mary?" Katryn asked.

"I guess I can visit Manhattan and not starve; I eat the same foods as them, city people," Mary answered.

"Mary, let me try to answer your question about transportation. In a big city, walking from Central Park, located in the middle of town, to the beach would be difficult, and it would take too long and tire a person out. So, New Yorkers travel by horse-drawn carriages or something of a group convenience called a trolley on a track, pulled by horses, which can accommodate ten or more people inside," Katryn explained.

"I can see how the organization of streets, a speed limit, and a poop patrol can play an important part in efficiency and safety in a big city. I guess the streets would have to be hosed down with soapy water daily for health concerns and clean-smelling air," Timothy analyzed.

"I can see the need for many people to work all sorts of important jobs, and it appears that when a city is as large as Manhattan, many workers are needed to fill all types of employment," Papa said.

"Papa, I can live in New York, attend Columbia, and work my way through college by working in a fancy hotel where I would get room and board for taking care of the horses that pull the hotel's carriages. What do you think, Mama?" Timothy asked.

"I don't know, Son. It's up to Papa. Whatever he says is okay with me," she answered.

"Well, I want a lawyer in our family, Mama, so it is fine with me," Papa answered.

"Well, I am glad that's settled," Katryn said.

"Now, who would like to draw a second map of New York and its five boroughs and the rivers?"

"May I?" asked Papa, who loved to draw and had paid close attention to Katryn's map. With a gallon of enthusiasm, Papa started. "Here is Manhattan, Brooklyn, Queens, Staten Island, and the Bronx. And here are the three rivers that are nearby: the Hudson, the East, and the Harlem. And they all empty into the Atlantic Ocean, right here," he illustrated.

"Perfect, Papa," Katryn said.

"Miss Katryn, would you show us your home?" asked little Zack.

"Absolutely! Here it is, Zack, on Park Avenue by Central Park. And over here is the Second Presbyterian Church, where I attend Sunday services. And down at the wharf, my father has a boat ramp with a forty-foot sloop ready to whisk us off after church for a Sunday sailboat ride with a box lunch."

"That sounds great, but it is time for prayers and bedtime. Lights go out at 7:00 p.m. for children and 9:00 p.m. for Mama and Papa," Lizbeth said.

Just like that, all the children, including her and Katryn, were in their beds by seven.

Mama and Papa went to bed by nine, but there was some pillow talk between them.

"Mama, our son Timothy is a smart boy. Bet he does go to New York, attend college, and become a lawyer. Maybe he'll be president of this here, United States. Who knows? Time will tell. Good night, my sweet love."

"Good night, dear husband. I love you too, and I think you are right about our son."

"Mama, can we have some of your wonderful strawberry crepes for breakfast?" Papa asked.

"Yes, dumpling!" Mama whispered in his ear. "I'll throw in some fried eggs, fat pork sausages, and dark rye toast. Please go to sleep; it will be 5:00 a.m. in no time."

Saturday Morning at 5:00

Katryn awoke before Mama and Lizbeth, but Timothy was already in the kitchen eating Mama's triple chocolate chip oatmeal cookies and drinking hot cocoa. He finished packing two peanut butter and grape jelly sandwiches on dark rye bread. He also brought along a jug of buttermilk, a dozen of last night's dessert cookies, and four fresh apples from the cold cellar for good measure.

Katryn quietly dressed. She slithered down the oak staircase and opened the white kitchen door with brass handles. She was on her way to meet Timothy but was overtaken by surprise when she saw him packing lunch.

"Timothy, fancy meeting Your Lordship here," she said humorously.

"I just wanted to prepare a snack for us until breakfast," he answered.

Suddenly the kitchen door swung open, and a familiar voice asked where Katryn and Timothy were going riding.

"Mother, fancy meeting you at this time of day. What are you up to?" Timothy asked.

"Your father wants me to make my famous prizewinning strawberry and whipped cream crepes, so don't be a minute late. Set the horses' time clock so they will turn around and head straight back here; breakfast will be served promptly at 9:00 a.m."

"Oh, I honestly feel horrible. I am leaving you to do all the work, Mama," Katryn said.

Mother assured her that Lizbeth would help her by preparing the crepe mixture once she'd milked the cow. Then Mama would add ten ounces of milk, one cup of flour, and four eggs together. After adding an ounce of butter, she would whisk the mixture together and pour some onto a hot skillet, two hefty tablespoons at a time.

"And I will fill the crepes with the magic strawberry jam I made last summer," Mama said with a pleased smile. "Then I will sprinkle powdered sugar on top of each crepe, fold into fours, and add the jam and whipped cream on top with a little peppermint on the side for garnish."

"Mama," Lizbeth promptly interrupted as she walked toward the kitchen door.

"Good morning, Sister. Nice to see you so helpful at this hour of the morning," Timothy blurted out.

"I am going to milk the cow—my regular job on Saturday mornings. Also, Mama needs some milk for her blue-ribbon crepe batter."

Katryn rolled her baby-blue eyes at her roommate. A blunt thought popped into her clever head: *So much for a chaperone, girlfriend; I'll just have to wing it.*

As a bright orange and gold sunrise tickled their youthful cheeks, Timothy presented Katryn with her mount, Miss Eloise, a brown Thoroughbred with a long silky black tail and mane, frequently referred to as a bay in horse language. The master mounted his bay, and the two of them rode off down the gray trail and up two short grassy hills before disappearing into the lush velvet green forest. The trees were tall, and the sun crept onto the trail, leading the way.

"Please follow me, Katryn, for a pleasurable surprise; don't lag, or you will lose me. My horse Dusty Rose loves to run away when my whip hits her tail."

"Don't worry. I will gently kick my mount in her ribs. Gets them to run faster every time."

Katryn couldn't help wondering what surprise Timothy had in store for her. *Better not be a passionate encounter with a juicy tongue kiss and his hands touching my lady parts,* she thought as her cheeks blushed a deep sunset pink and her forehead furrowed into elevens. *That behavior just won't do. I do have my horsewhip, which I'll use if necessary.*

The horses suddenly stopped in a meadow filled with Virginia bluebells and yellowwood poppies. To Katryn's astonishment, she saw three other couples dressed in the same garb as she and Timothy, who were perched upon tan English leather saddles that had been recently polished, which made them glisten in the sunrays streaming through the tree branches above.

"Everyone, may I present my friend and Lizbeth's school roommate, Miss Katryn Kline Wellington, from New York City," Timothy exclaimed with excitement.

"And, Katryn, may I introduce the Klugers, the Schultzes, and the Schmidts, who all have farms in the vicinity of my home and are very good friends of mine. We all have something in common. Every Saturday morning, we meet here in the meadow and hunt for a particularly rare bird that we draw in our notebooks once we find it. The first couple to see it wins a picnic basket filled with wine, cheese, bread, and fruit. We don't believe in hunting foxes or rabbits; that is too cruel," Timothy explained to Katryn.

"I understand. And you weren't kidding when you talked about a surprise ride. I am very impressed! Thank you so much for inviting me, Timothy. Everyone's horses are so beautiful and very elegant, standing tall with their tails sashaying in the wind. I am delighted to make all your acquaintances."

"Likewise," they all murmured.

"Well, we'd better get started," exclaimed Timothy. "Today's bird is the *Bubo virginianus*, better known as the great horned owl or tiger owl. Look for a thick body with an undertone of white- to buff-colored feathers that are imbued with darker shades of brown, gray-brown, or black-brown. The wings are broad and rounded, their eyes are yellow, and their hoot is deep sounding. Are there any questions?" Timothy asked for Katryn's benefit.

"Get ready, get set, *go*!" he shouted.

Off they went, walking and trotting, looking for their prey. Timothy took Katryn on another path, one that led to the right. Suddenly they heard a deep-sounding hoot. They looked up to behold a nest of screaming owlets hanging from a branch that was about to break. Mama bird was nowhere to be found. Oops!

"Look, they are going to fall to their demise any second!" Katryn cried.

"I can see that. Wait! I have an idea to save them." He pointed to the stronger branch just six inches above the owlets' heads and decided to cut his right saddlebag strap, stand on top of his horse, and attach the weak branch to the one above it with the leather strap, which would hold it in place forever.

"Timothy, it is a blessing that your horse is eighteen hands tall enough to accomplish your super creative idea. You rock in my book, even if your hair is sticking out all over!" Katryn chuckled. "Here is the picture I drew while you were saving the day," Katryn said.

Timothy gazed at it and saw that Katryn was a fantastic artist comparable to his sister Lizbeth. She had captured the entire rescue with accurate detail, and it helped them win the picnic basket.

Back at the farm and on time for breakfast, Timothy and Katryn were sitting around the table eating delicious crepes and watching everyone else admire the picture Katryn had drawn while listening to the most unbelievable horse story ever told.

There was a loud knock at the door, and Papa cried out for that person to enter. A tall, brown-haired, blue-eyed gentleman in his early twenties stood in the kitchen doorway. He turned out to be Lizbeth's boyfriend, Martin Bozemon, who lived five miles away on a pig farm.

"Good morning, Papa. I thought you would like one of my blue-ribbon sows that is going to give birth in a few weeks and a dozen cabbages to make sauerkraut. The sow won first prize at the fair last year for her lean, strong body and good teeth. I also brought you three of my best Clydesdale yearlings to help you pull your new wagon and tractor," Martin said. "You know there isn't anything I wouldn't do for you and your family to help you prosper."

"Thank you so much, Martin," Papa said with great appreciation. "Please sit down and have brunch with us. We're having Mama's famous strawberry crepes with eggs, fat spicy sausages, and country-fried buttered apples."

Martin thanked Mama and Papa for the delicious invitation and then sat down across from his beloved. His eyes just gazed at his future wife, Lizbeth, whom he had been dating for two years. They had met in church and attended many functions together where they danced and talked each other's ears off about their future together. They talked about where they would live, how many children they'd have, and how to convince her papa to give Martin permission to marry his favorite daughter.

Then one day about six weeks ago, two Mormon missionaries knocked on Martin's door. After six visits, he and Lizbeth were baptized and converted to the Church of Jesus Christ of Latter-day Saints. Her parents were in attendance; they believed a wife should take her husband's religion, and their children should follow suit. Because of this, there was no resistance from them, even though the two new Mormons were planning to move to the Utah Territory after Lizbeth graduated from Miss Hawthorne's Academy in June.

CHAPTER 4
THE HAUNTING MORMON PROPHECY

Two Years Later

It was here in Lancaster, Pennsylvania, that Katryn was introduced to the Mormon religion through Lizbeth, who later married Martin Bozemon, a pillar of the Mormon faith. Together they migrated west in a Conestoga wagon, where they joined the Prophet Brigham Young and other church members in Utah Territory. One day, Lizbeth wrote Katryn a long letter describing how great life was in this pure, righteous, God-fearing religion and how the women were treated with great respect. Lizbeth also explained how their influence was integral to her family's salvation. She always encouraged Katryn to join them as soon as possible. Lizbeth always added at the end of her letters that many eligible bachelors were searching for righteous wives, but they weren't going to last much longer; women were migrating to Salt Lake from England on a daily basis—"Like twenty-five a day, so hurry up out here, girlfriend, *pronto!*"

Katryn had other plans—this one fiancé had died mysteriously—but she always enjoyed reading Lizbeth's letters. She was having too much fun in New York with several gentlemen and traveling throughout Europe to drop everything for one man. Moving to a primitive wilderness like Utah Territory was not her cup of tea either. She was accustomed to indoor plumbing; gaslights; luxurious clothes made from the finest linens and furs; feathered chapeaus and ball gowns from Paris; diamonds, rubies, and emeralds from India and South Africa; and classical music and art direct from Austria and Paris. And the operas and Broadway plays were unmatchable.

One evening as Katryn returned home from the opera, she heard a familiar voice in the study. *Could it be Papa?* she thought. As she walked toward that elegant English accent, she saw the handsome figure of her father standing with perfect posture, dressed in an English gray tweed riding suit and britches. As she called out, "Father, Father," Katryn ran into the duke's long arms and kissed him on his rosy cheek.

He returned the kiss on her forehead and whispered, "I love you, my little princess. Daddy is home now to take care of you."

Katryn just melted in his embrace and felt safe again. Her best friend in the whole world, who loved Katryn more than he loved any of his horses and possessions, was here for her once again. *But will he let me be myself? I have grown older and wiser and have experienced more about life than when he was last home,* Katryn thought with worry.

The butler rang the dinner bell at 9:00 p.m. sharp, and a cold pheasant supper with potato salad and pickled beets with an assortment of wines—Riesling, claret, and champagne—was served. A strong, smooth English sherry and upside-down pineapple cake followed the meal.

Yes, the duke finally had returned from India with a lust for living grand. He was determined to erase the poor, wretched, and miserable living conditions he had experienced in India for the past ten difficult years. So, wasting not a precious moment, Katryn's father moved his duchess and daughter into his parents' spacious, luxurious mansion. It had a white-tiled fireplace in every room—located on Long Island Sound, where the soft foamy curls of ocean water beating on the shore could be heard between the summer breezes. The impetuous cultured duke also bought an art museum specializing in fine High Renaissance pieces—Da Vinci, Raphael, Michelangelo, and Botticelli—which were the rage in the rich circles among the sacred elite of New York City. Afterward, the duke sold his big Park Avenue home, where Frenchie and Katryn had lived in his absence, for a cozy brownstone on Madison Avenue near the famous Central Park, where his daughter could ride English and go boating and ice-skating on the lake. In addition to purchasing more property, the Duke of Wellington and Frenchie had two more children—fraternal twin boys Jacob and Joseph. They wanted to give Katryn siblings so she would never feel alone once they spiritually departed. The duke had raised the boys to watch over their sister, who was impetuous like him and would always need guidance, being a woman and all. But he quickly discovered his impression of her was wrong. Katryn proved herself to be brilliant in business and a solid force to reckon with. Her sense of honor, like her father's, could not be broken.

The duke wanted to get to know his daughter better and guide her to choose the proper husband. He knew there were many suitors who were only interested in her irresistible beauty, a considerable inheritance, and a very handsome dowry that he had placed in a trust fund for only her use, not her future husband's. Katryn's father wanted to help her choose the best candidate among the elite Sacred Four Hundred and marry well. After her coming-out party at the Waldorf Astoria in Manhattan, Katryn was courted by many eligible bachelors of the most influential families of New York. She received many proposals and rejected them all, breaking many hearts and making her father drink too much. Her choice of a husband just wasn't in the mundane and the predictable and carbon copies of the usual Harvard and Yale graduate aspiring to become a wealthy lawyer or doctor, which would always receive her father's approval.

On the contrary, Katryn wanted no part of the Sacred Four Hundred and their money; she considered them peacocks, hypocrites, and boring. The men Lizbeth described in her letters piqued her interest more. All Katryn wanted was to be free to choose if, when, where, and whom she would marry. Katryn didn't believe in divorce because parent separations hurt children's sense of security. She believed absence doesn't make the heart grow fonder when children can't see either parent daily. She had a heart of gold and lots of common sense. The man she chose would be her king, and she would be his queen for all eternity.

"But, Katryn," the duke said to his daughter, "you have many interesting suitors since your performance at church." Katryn's classical piano Christmas recital, the first movement of Beethoven's *Moonlight* Sonata, captured the hearts of everyone who heard her play. "Darling, you were positively superb at capturing Beethoven's exquisite style. Your grace, elegance, and hefty dowry are a huge temptation for any gentleman. The right one will come along. And soon! Just be patient," he urged her as an inspiring father should.

But only the honorable would do for Katryn. She wanted someone who loved the Lord more than her money, someone with cerebral substance and wit who would understand her independent thinking and make her laugh.

For a moment, Katryn pondered her beaux. There was Clyde Barker, who owned a circus and took her out to plays and steak suppers. He loved her independence; she loved his baby tigers. Katryn named all three: Jasper, Conan, and Jezebel. Then there was Josiah Randal, a first cousin to John Jacob Astor. He was an accountant for Astor's holdings in Europe and wanted to take Katryn there for a honeymoon. Another prospect was Peter Vanderbilt, nephew to the great railroad tycoon Cornelius Vanderbilt. Peter was smitten with her because of her stand on women's issues. Like his mother, Katryn was for legal and medical education for women and women's right to vote and advocated for abortion only to save the life of the mother, promoting adoption as an alternative. He knew that her positions on these issues were ahead of her time. He admired her convictions and accepted her thoughts unequivocally and unconditionally, which is why Katryn preferred Peter over all her other beaux. But he had one huge drawback—he professed to be an atheist. And after having read Lizbeth's letters describing Mormon thought, Katryn wanted something different in a husband. She just couldn't get those letters out of her pretty head, especially the one about finding "the righteous one" who would be there for her during childbirth, holding her hand.

Katryn was ready for marriage. She slept with Lizbeth's letter under her pillow every night and prayed to the Lord to send her such a man. Over and over, she would read the part describing how Mormon men treated their wives and children and the righteous one who would protect her and be there for her during childbirth. Next to this image, all her other suitors' aptitudes for making good husbands appeared trivial and weak. It was difficult for Katryn to find one ounce of courage in any of their bodies. And the way they dressed was ridiculous—looking like pompous dilettantes waiting to have their eyebrows plucked. Katryn hated how they always worried about their reputations, curled mustaches, and stocks. She was exaggerating, but nevertheless, she was smitten with Lizbeth's friend, the Mormon cowboy, whose name Lizbeth had failed to tell her.

Katryn Kline Wellington was no pushover. She knew men inside and out—from the brothel days—and what made their brains tick: sex, money, and power, in that order. A soft wind was blowing from the west as she sat on her front porch sipping mint tea. She heard horses pulling a stagecoach; it was the postman who brought her two letters that came from out west somewhere. Upon opening it, Katryn saw it was from Lizbeth Bozemon, who explained that Brigham Young was in jail and awaiting trial. *Life has suddenly taken a turn for the worse for the Mormons,* Katryn thought.

The second letter read as follows:
Dear Katryn,

I hope you and your family are doing well. Something terrible has happened. Please don't think of coming to visit me yet. The Prophet Brigham was shot in his shoulder but is still alive; we are all moving west to a safer Zion. Gentile mobs are running wild, burning and looting houses and stealing livestock and precious belongings like photo albums and genealogy records that can never be replaced. They even burned the printing press where the Book of Mormon was being reprinted in Salt Lake. Life is going haywire; it is not safe to be here. You must wait until we have moved southwest to St. George and have a safer home before you stay with us. Perhaps next year.

Those Gentile cowards have killed innocent women, children, and helpless pets. Gentiles are not to be trusted, Katryn. Our two-story home in Salt Lake burned down right in front of us. It was terrible; I fainted. When I came to, I was in our buggy going to God knows where. Not all the Mormons left, which I didn't understand. I guess they were tired of losing their farms like before and had decided to stand their ground, protecting what God had helped them build. They are probably pushing up daisies as I write this letter. So please don't come yet. I promise when we get settled again, I will write you. Katryn, a war is coming; I feel it in my bones. There is just too much bickering and hatred toward God's chosen people. Martin says it will be between the states that practice slavery and those that don't. The North versus the South, brother against brother, cousin against cousin, and so forth. But I say it will be with Mexico. But what do I know? I am just an innocent woman who understands world events. Thank God, Mr. Plowshare taught us to read something other than scripture. Current events were our favorite; we dreamed of going to San Francisco to find rich husbands. What foolish dreams we had back then when life was simple!

On the lighter side, Katryn, I discovered once you have children in the Mormon Church, you are like some Madonna sitting high on a pedestal overlooking dirty dishes, washing soiled clothes, darning socks, and raising nine to eighteen children to work the fields and plows. And later, they will go on a Mormon mission, marry, and raise a family, starting the blessed Mormon cycle all over again. I love my life!

My sweet friend, please be happy while you can, and don't marry anyone but a righteous man who loves the Lord with his every breath. Make sure he will be a good provider and will help during childbirth instead of running off to the nearest bar or house—you know what I mean.

Well, I have run out of things to say, sweet friend. God bless you! Until we meet again.

Your faithful friend,
Lizbeth

Katryn ran into the house. She had made up her mind to move west and decided to study the two M's, music and Mormonism, before leaving for parts unknown—the challenging and mysterious West. She was lucky to find some Mormon missionaries to visit her at home once a week to read the Book of Mormon. Katryn wanted to be well-versed in Mormonism before she met the one. Days passed, then weeks, and then months. Before long, a year had passed, and Katryn was ready to become a Mormon, but she preferred to wait until she went to Utah Territory.

As part of a daily routine, Katryn watched for a letter from Lizbeth, but nothing came. She was just sick with worry that perhaps her sweet friend and her family had met a terrible fate.

"Miss Katryn," said Lilly, her maid, "a letter came for you last week, but I put it up and then couldn't find it. It disappeared. It's the leprechauns, you know; they are prone to hiding your treasured belongings and then dropping them anywhere they please. I found it this morning."

"Right." Katryn chuckled. "Leprechauns!"

Katryn grabbed the letter with enthusiasm and ran up the stairs to her bedroom, where she locked the door. She knew this letter was going to be important and wanted to read it without any interruptions.

My Dearest Friend Katryn,

I am a mother. God blessed Martin and me with two beautiful twin girls, Sara, and Mary Lu. They do not look alike, which is okay because they are perfect in every other way. To my amazement, we all finally made it to a safer Zion, and I do not think we will ever move again. It is in Mexican territory, due west several hundred miles from Denver, Colorado, which is due west from Missouri. The best thing is that we are basically alone and can practice the principle without Gentile and government interference. You are the only Gentile besides my parents I trust.

Since my last letter, many Mormon men perished either by protecting their families or dying on the trek to Zion. Believe me; it was worth the wait. You can actually feel the Lord's majestic presence amid a great basin of purple sage and several lakes filled with many fish, where wild game abounds, such as deer, antelope, and elk. There is also this magical lake with abundant salt in it, and it looks just like the Atlantic Ocean with blue water. Inside this lake, the Indians have found many shrimp and other fish. It is truly remarkable to find shrimp way out here in the high desert, don't you think, Katryn?

The Lord's presence is strong and definitive out here, and you can feel him wherever you go throughout this wilderness. Our new prophet, Brigham Young, led us here because the Lord guided him to what has become our final destination. Here we will build a temple like no other and attract many converts. The ground is fertile for planting wheat and corn, and the mountains have an abundance of snow, providing water in the springtime. Also, the streams and rivers have delicious fish to catch. What makes fish delicious is how I fry it in corn oil. Sometimes I stuff it with shrimp from the Great Salt Lake and herbs from the meadows and use a flour coating with Mexican spices.

We have met many Indians who have taught us how to cultivate this new land, and in return, we have nursed their sick and taught them how to speak English and read the Book of Mormon in English. Brigham asked all of us not to push our religion on them. Their conversion will come voluntarily after they know how to read and write English. Through our kind deeds, we will win them over.

Oh, Katryn, life out here is very different and challenging. There are no stores or towns nearby. We have become planters. We bake our own bread, milk goats and cows, pluck feathers from fowl, and store jerky, flour, and water for many months. I have become a great canner. There is a woman's organization called the Relief Society I belong to. We help each other when babies or death, or sickness comes. We share recipes and help each other tie quilts. Life is better shared than struggling alone, I believe.

Our men are too busy tending their ranches, hunting, or doing missionary work to pay us, wives, much attention. All we do is minister to each other for the Lord's sake. And it all evens out at some point.

Guess what, girlfriend? I met the perfect man for you. He is tall, blond, and very handsome with piercing blue eyes and rich and righteous. Perfect! Also, he is an experienced lover with two former wives and one adorable daughter, Lizette. So hurry up and get out here. I can use your help with the girls. And surprise! There is a new one on the way. I am just a beautiful baby-making machine. What can I say?

The Transcontinental Railroad is now running east to west and west to east. Hop on the train and be here in one week, tops. Martin and I will meet you at the train station in Salt Lake City. No more wagons or pushcarts.

Godspeed!
—Lizbeth and the gang

PS: Don't forget to telegraph me when you will arrive. Martin and I will meet you. And please don't bring a bunch of clothes. We do not have a washing machine yet. That means, if you haven't guessed, we must use our hands and brawn. And Martin says he only does men's work, so we are on our own. Just like a man! Ha-ha!

CHAPTER 5
THOMAS

Before Katryn and wife number two were in his life, a sandy-haired Mormon named Thomas used to stir up the young women's blood when he walked into Sunday school with what he called his woman. With a catching Sunday attire—a crisp white ironed shirt, silver and coral bolo, turquoise-studded cufflinks, navy-blue trousers, and a medium brown leather belt topped with a four-inch-by-four-inch Native American–made shiny silver buckle with the initials T. H. carved on the front. His medium brown leather boots were polished and smelled fresh. He always wore a lavender astringent on his face after shaving to tighten his pores. The women simply were intoxicated by his "so sure of himself" attitude. He knew he was the most dignified blue-eyed peacock this side of Nauvoo, Illinois. Women would just fall at his feet, hoping to become the next Mrs. Huntzmon, have a ridiculous number of perfect babies, and be rich with maids, furs, jewelry, and fancy clothes from Paris. So whenever he was near a woman, she would drop her dainty handkerchief of white lace, hoping he would pick it up, so she could work her charms with her long curly eyelashes and invite him for Sunday supper. He shocked them all when he ignored their attempts and married a Jewish woman from New York named Katryn Kline Wellington. But that happens later in the story.

For the second time, Thomas, now a Mormon widower, followed a strict righteous code of behavior. He decided he would relax once he married his third wife, Katryn after she converted from Judaism. His parents had wondered if he would ever take a third wife. But Thomas assured them he would. The Lord had promised him in his patriarchal blessing—performed by the ward patriarch in the future—that he would have many children to go forth as missionaries and spread the principle and Mormon dogma.

"Of course, I will marry again, Mother. I need someone to take care of little Lizette and me. I must keep the principle alive. I promised Father," Thomas offered.

"Just make sure you marry a Mormon. No Gentiles permitted in this family," his father, Martin, ranted from the parlor.

"You yelled so loudly that even the horses and cows heard you." Martin's wife, Esther, chuckled.

"Please stop worrying. I will obey the Lord and follow the Prophet's counsel given to him by God," thirty-two-year-old Thomas had responded to his dutiful parents. "When I find someone to marry, I will know if she is worthy of the Huntzmon name. My humble heart loves deeply and tenderly, and I would never want to scare a new bride off with strict church practices like plural marriage, especially if she is pretty and appears malleable. Not everyone practices or believes in polygamy at first, Mother and Dad. Very few Mormon men have the financial means to support more than one wife, let alone another houseful of eighteen or more children. Besides, it is best to ease my new bride into sharing my religious belief of plural marriage after our fourth child is born. Don't you agree?"

Thomas's parents both nodded their heads yes, even though they refused to follow the principle. Esther refused to share Martin.

"This thing called polygamy is a passing fancy," she would always say when the subject came up.

"It is best, I feel, to wait for when the bride is older and for a time when a second pair of hands will become welcome to assist with extra domestic and child-rearing chores."

"Good strategy, Son," Martin Huntzmon added.

"Thanks for the compliment, Dad. Hearing your approval of my plans makes me overjoyed with delight."

Thomas didn't want to disappoint his church or his father, who was as strict as they came in Mormon Utah Territory. Moreover, Brigham Young had personally asked Thomas to take more wives and produce more saints to propagate the principle of plural marriage.

"All good things come to those who follow the scriptures and are patient. Remember, the Lord's timetable is different from yours, and he is worth waiting for. Keep him in your thoughts and pray frequently, and he will never fail you," Brigham Young once told Thomas, who had never forgotten the Prophet's wise words. Thomas just diligently kept working hard on the ranch and trusted the Lord to send him his next wife.

Life on the Ranch

The first thing Thomas did every morning of work was meet with his foreman, Cleaver, over a powerful breakfast of ham steaks with fried potatoes, yellow onions mixed with red pepper flakes, and scrambled eggs inside a large tortilla. A giant cinnamon bun followed by Pear juice and hot chocolate. Thoroughly over breakfast, they discussed the day's work schedule to assess the number of cows, horses, and sheep Thomas owned and identify which fences needed mending. Cleaver would then send the cowboys out over Huntzmon Valley accordingly. On the north forty, some of the cowboys wrangled horses, while other ranch hands to the south counted pairs of cows and calves. And to the west, some cowboys mended fences down by the lake. Thomas loved his ranch and often pondered how safe it was to live in Mormon country; most of the time, the pioneers were free from rustlers, murderers, and the P-word—Mormon persecution by the Gentiles. So much for the United States Constitution, which listed religious freedom as an inalienable, guaranteed right given by God. But life didn't work out that way for God's chosen people. The Mormons were killed, tortured, and raped; they had their homes burned or stolen by the United States government or Gentiles. Eventually were driven out of three states, Illinois, Indiana, and Missouri, because of their strange religious beliefs that threatened everyone else's political, religious, and economic beliefs. Simply said, Mormons produced many voters and stuck together in a voting bloc, thus becoming a massive threat to determining whether a state was a free state or a slave state. The Mormons had settled in Council Bluffs, Iowa, before finding their way to Zion, now called Utah Territory, Mexico. The highly persecuted Mormons had to suffer from shock, exhaustion, and fear of the United States governments and Gentiles' relentless persecution.

Once in Utah Territory, the Mormon militia was formed to protect Mormons and their property. The Mormons quickly made friends with the local Natives on the basis that the Natives were ancestors of the Latter-day Saints, whose scriptures had come with Jewish tribes from Israel—the Laminites, Nephites, and Jaredites—who migrated to this country back in 600 BC. So, on this strong basis of kinship and mutual hatred of the United States, a beautiful, loyal, and strong friendship was born between Mormons and Native Americans.

The Mormons taught the Natives to read and write English and farm with modern techniques, and they converted many Natives to their faith. On the other side, the Natives taught the Mormons how to survive in the wilderness by sharing which mushrooms and berries were okay to eat, which wild herbs cured what ailments, and how to hunt and fish as no other American could. Some Mormon men even married Native women. Soon, there were many Native converts to the LDS Church.

Life was grand for ten years in Zion, but then came "big trouble"—the Mexican-American War of 1852. Zion became a territory of the United States. The Mormons would not run this time but would either stand their ground or perish. They trusted the Lord that they would not lose, which they didn't. They all remembered how, back in Nauvoo, their cattle had been stolen on a regular basis, and they'd left everything behind thrice. But this time, there would be no more running away in Zion. *Enough is enough!* They all thought.

There in the wilderness, miles away from US civilization, for ten years, the Mormons felt that life was paradise—smooth sailing all the way to the slaughterhouse, the bank, and of course, the supper table. Having a day off the ranch was the highlight of a ranch hand's life. He valued meeting with family and friends and looking for fun on his days off. Ranching was never boring; there was always some drama with the cows, giving birth in the weirdest places—under a bog or on a mountaintop, far away from the other cows—or getting their feet caught in barbed wire, which could prove fatal if a mountain lion were to pass by. Keeping the herd alive till the market was a challenge. That is why Thomas and the men would pray daily on their knees before and after they labored for twelve hours, the standard length of their workday.

The property around the ranch had many dangerous critters that could kill a cow in no time. The mountain lion attacked the neck first to bring down its prey; then, she devoured the rest after breaking off some meat for her cubs. A grizzly bear was different; he chased his prey until he killed it and left it lying when he was done. Mama bear had no trouble finding food for her young, who mostly ate fish and berries. Other critters like the beaver could stop the water flow and kill crops with their mighty dams. Snakes could turn a horse sideways and backward until it fell and broke something serious. The skunks and raccoons were just troublesome little devils. You started to hate them when your pie had no sweetness to it. They loved to steal sugar in all its forms—cubed or granulated. And sometimes, a pack rat would get into the house and steal something shiny like a diamond ring, silver bracelet, or gold watch, which you'd never find it again, having embarrassed yourself by accusing your family members of stealing your valuables. Life was never dull working on a ranch. And a day off was a treasure to a cowboy.

Another chore for a hired hand was to clean and polish his rifle and six-shooter daily. This kept it ready to go during any surprise attack, such as an unfriendly Native American war party passing by to steal horses. Thomas was a stickler for being prepared for any occasion. He took great pains to hire the best men in the county, and he paid them more money than any other rancher did and kept them well-fed at breakfast time—the most important meal for a wrangler. Plus, every Christmas, they each received a $500 bonus.

Cleaver, Thomas's foreman, worried about his boss's well-being. He knew Thomas was at his best when he had a wife to look after him, preparing biscuits and gravy, hot cakes, and thick juicy ham steaks for breakfast. Having a kid or two didn't hurt either, and marriage just gave his boss purpose and satisfaction following the principle of plural marriage. It didn't hurt Cleaver any either; he ate breakfast with Thomas every morning to discuss ranch business. Wasn't he lucky?

"Thomas, my boy, aren't you tired of eating toast and your mother's last Christmas jam? When are you getting married again?" Cleaver asked.

"I'm working on it. It's just that it is so busy here and at church. Brigham has me traveling with my father two nights a week. I have been looking for a righteous, pretty woman at church," Thomas said with a gleaming eye and a chuckle.

"Have you now? I see your eyes mostly shut during sacrament meetings and scripture time. You have to flirt with the ladies to get their attention," Cleaver added.

"Oh, shucks, Cleaver, I am tired; besides, to be honest, there isn't a woman who has caught my fancy yet."

"No?" Cleaver asked.

"That's right, a big, fat double *no*! The woman I want must have something special to offer me, like exotic eyes and shiny blonde hair. And I will know her at first glance. The minute our eyes meet, she will faint into my arms, and then I will wake her with my tender kiss," Thomas teased.

The two men burst out in roaring laughter, nearly upchucking their breakfasts. Twenty minutes later, they galloped off to the hills with a bright warm sun shining on their tanned faces, looking for stray cattle. Thomas had a slightly hairy muscled chest and a smooth, curved back. He looked majestic and kingly in a light blue open shirt, brown cotton pants, and a dark brown cowboy hat, sitting tall and upright in his brown leather saddle atop the prize-coveted Indian pony he had raised from a foal. One of Thomas's Paiute friends, Brave Eagle, gave her to him as a trade for a knife made from unbreakable material only found in Germany that Thomas had inherited from his mother's grandfather, Isaac Campbell from Scotland.

Thomas was thirty-two and had two wives, Kirstin and Lizette, who died during childbirth. Their hips were too narrow, and their feminine parts were stretched and ripped open to get the babies out. They just couldn't take the pain and lost a great deal of blood. Kirstin's baby, a boy, was choked to death by the umbilical cord, while Lizette's baby girl miraculously lived. Her cord, not as tight, was carefully removed from around her tiny neck by an intelligent, experienced midwife.

Old wives rumored that woman with wide hips had many babies that lived. But both his wives had been the prettiest girls around St. George and very young too—fourteen and fifteen, respectively. He couldn't resist and fell in love at first sight.

By the time a wife turned forty-eight, she was considered by her husband to be old meat after having nine or eighteen kids. And a man always wanted to feel that young, fresh womanhood rubbing on him at night and to enjoy the pleasures of feeling his manhood enlarge and explode from such cherished firmness. Holding a newborn baby in one's arms nine months later was a feeling like no other. God is great, God is good, and God loves lots of babies!

That evening, after a hard day's work of branding cows, Thomas put six-month-old Lizette to bed and softly whispered in her ear, "I promise you, my little dumpling, I will bring home a new mother who will love you forever and stick around for a long time because she is going to have wide hips. I swear it on Joseph Smith's grave! Also, I had a vision when I was praying, and the Lord said it will be so. For, you see, my little Liebchen, your new mama will be here soon. And she will love you for all eternity. She is going to sing to you, cook your porridge, squeeze the goats' teats for your milk, sew your dresses, wash and iron your clothes, teach you to sing and dance, and teach you to read and write your name and to add and subtract figures. She will be a great mama, by gosh; you wait and see! She will be here by Christmas, I promise. The Lord said so! Once we are all sealed in the temple, you will have three mothers to love you. For now, the sisters of the St. George Relief Society will watch over us and take good care of you like you were their very own baby girl."

In the Mormon Church, there was a sisterhood group called the

Women's Relief Society. It was founded by Emma Smith, who was married to the Prophet Joseph Smith back in Nauvoo, Illinois. He contributed church funds and helped make it a great service organization. The purpose of this sisterhood was to help families of the church who were destitute, orphaned, or widowed or who needed any benevolent services, especially during marriages, births, sickness, and deaths. The women helped by cooking; baking; nursing; cleaning; washing, ironing, and mending clothes; babysitting; and, in some instances contributing money. They held many cake fundraisers. Joseph Smith was known to offer five dollars in solid gold coins for a prized cake his wife Emma made.

And so, the story went those two sisters from the Relief Society were assigned to care for Thomas and little Lizette. Every morning like clockwork, one of the women would show up at 6:00 a.m. sharp and prepare breakfast for Thomas, his foreman, and baby Lizette. Thomas tied Sadie the goat to the porch for proximity to squeeze fresh milk from her teats for the baby before the sisters came. After kissing little Lizette on her plump rosy cheeks, Thomas would gather up Cleaver and ride out to cowpunch—a term used to describe herding cattle to another part of the ranch to graze or be branded. In this case, the goal was to brand each cow and heifer with the Huntzmon brand, so they could be easily matched to Thomas if they strayed. Thomas's favorite dog, Casey, was a multicolored crossbreed who slept on his bed nightly, protecting Thomas from danger. Thomas claimed she was part Australian shepherd and part dingo. Both breeds were bred to protect livestock. It just came naturally to Casey to care for Lizette when she crawled. She stayed with her in the yard, and sometimes when Thomas whistled, she would grab the baby by her clothes and carry her into the house. The perfect nanny!

Another favorite person in Thomas's life was his father, Martin, one of Brigham Young's right-hand men and trustee to the Mormon Church's financial records, which included a secret map. He held many secrets and could only pass this job down to his only son, Thomas, who had no clue the power he would one day possess to pass down to his son and so forth. Martin taught his son how to ride, shoot, fish, pray, work hard, and catch a wife. Keeping a wife happy in the bedroom was another skill he taught Thomas, something all

Mormon fathers did to ensure their good name and fertile genes were perpetuated. They relied on God to bring them through adversity and challenges, which they understood would only strengthen their faith and resolve and give them many blessings in this life and the next. Thomas and his family were very close and relied on each other for moral support during difficult times. And the more Huntzmons there were, the better chance of leaving a true Mormon legacy, one that was righteous and pleasing to the Lord and provided many more saints and missionaries to proselytize the principle throughout the world.

CHAPTER 6
UTAH TERRITORY

Katryn's train pulled into the Salt Lake station on a cold, sunny day in December of 1870; Martin, Lizbeth, and all the kids were waiting for her. Determined to make her feel welcome, the Mormon Tabernacle Choir—at the request of an enormous donor with the initials M. H.—was there singing Christmas carols to welcome the new convert.

"Wow! I don't know what to say, guys. I feel like a princess," Katryn exclaimed with her regal dimpled smile as she warmly hugged her two friends from Pennsylvania.

"Well, you are my best friend, and I will do anything to help you stay here and find the one," replied Lizbeth, who had a big devilish grin on her pretty face, which was enveloped by long, reddish-brown curls.

"Okay, who is he?" asked Katryn. "I can tell that you already have someone in mind for me, Lizbeth; your hazel eyes are sparkling. I must know, who is this perfect specimen?"

Lizbeth wore a smile that seemed to stretch from California to New York. She took a very deep breath. "Well, there is this one brother who is very loyal to the church and comes from a righteous family. His father, Martin, is in the First Presidency and worked alongside Joseph Smith in Palmyra, New York, at the printing press where the first Book of Mormon was printed. Remember, this brother has one little girl and is a widower. He sees that there is money to feed the poor in our ward—similar to a parish. And, oh yes." Lizbeth chuckled. "There is a tiny character flaw: Thomas has good business sense, which has made him the wealthiest cattle baron in all Utah Territory."

The sun was bright that cold day in December as the friends got into their carriage and headed to St. George, about a three-day trip. *Katryn's rosy cheeks, ruby-red lips, and angelic face will captivate Thomas,* thought Lizbeth. *But her clothes are all wrong—too French! I will have to do something about that. I will just have to make her some gingham riding skirts and blouses with cute brown suede vests.*

"So, tell me more about Thomas Huntzmon," Katryn said.

"Well, he just lost his second wife to childbirth and is looking for wife number three to help raise little Lizette. Also, he has a dry sense of humor that is childlike, dresses casually in dark pants and plaid shirts, and is a devoted father and husband. Is that enough detail, my friend?"

Katryn shook her head, which indicated she was satisfied with Lizbeth's description of her future husband. *You bet I am interested. He sounds like the one,* Katryn thought with hidden exaltation in her bursting heart.

"What is his mother like? Men always want to marry their mothers."

"That is a brilliant question. His wonderful mother, Esther Marie—kin to John D. Lee—is from Virginia and cooks the tastiest fried chicken, mashed potatoes, and smooth white gravy I've ever eaten. Her fried okra is also good—never slimy. And her chocolate coconut seven-layer cake with raspberry filling is to die for. I know what you are thinking, Katryn."

"What am I thinking, missy?"

"You're thinking, *Just where do you get coconut all the way out here?* Brigham Young has everything at his store in Salt Lake, and I hear it comes from the island called Hawaii, which is in the Pacific Ocean, where one of his sons did a mission."

"Hawaii? I must visit one day. Perhaps on my honeymoon," Katryn said, chuckling, "as Mrs. Thomas Huntzmon."

She stared out the coach window with her baby blues and shook her head as her blonde tresses cascaded to the left side of her angelic face when she turned and looked at Lizbeth head-on. Without hesitation, Katryn asked, "Does Thomas dance?"

"You bet he dances. One of the best in Santa Clara County. Second to my husband, of course. There is going to be a Christmas ball—Thomas always attends—at our stake center in two weeks, just enough time to make you a red velvet ball gown, your best color, that will knock his socks off!"

"Where do you get red velvet out here in the wilderness, Lizbeth? Let me guess, Brigham's store?"

"Yes, and he gets it from the Montgomery Ward catalog."

"I am impressed," replied Katryn. "I can't wait to meet the one."

"Hush up, darling. Do you want to get excommunicated?" asked Martin.

"What does that grotesque word mean, Lizbeth?"

"Tell you later, alligator," she said.

"After a while, crocodile," replied Katryn.

They both burst into a fit of laughter, just like they used to do back at Miss Hawthorne's Academy in Pennsylvania.

Martin laughed at them and then began to sing softly to himself. Girl talk always bored him. He was more of a man's man into ranching and hunting. He made a wonderful husband and father. He believed in polygamy and knew he had to take a second wife soon to promote the principle. He dreaded the thought of telling his wife he had met number two in Brigham's Cedar City store last month during the Thanksgiving season when he was looking at gingham fabric and leather to make some dresses, shirts, and belts for the kids—skills he learned from his mother. Sisters weren't always around when you really needed them. *I'll get around to it sooner rather than later,* Martin pondered. Brigham had been pressuring all the men to follow suit. He had many wives and went around the Utah Territory with his favorite wife, Amelia, spreading the positives of the principle of plural marriage.

The morning after the group arrived at the Bozemon ranch, Katryn awoke to a beautifully warm and sunny day. She heard the birds chirping in the front yard. Suddenly there was a knock on her spacious, rosebud-wallpapered bedroom door. In walked the maid, O'Reilly, with a huge silver tray of homemade delicacies: freshly squeezed pear juice; apple fritters; a soft-boiled egg in a pretty small cup; strawberry jam on toast; a bowl of oatmeal layered with a natural cream, raisins, brown sugar, and honey; and a mug of hot cocoa with a dab of whipped cream to wash everything down.

After Katryn ate a little bit of everything, she took a hot bath in a white Victorian bathtub. To assist with bathing were small, dainty pink-colored soaps; vanilla-scented bath salts from Paris; a small silver hand mirror; hot wax and linen strips plied with honey to remove unwanted facial hair around the upper lips; and English lavender shampoo to be rinsed with a lemon-scented solution to condition her blonde locks.

After all this fuss, Katryn and Lizbeth rode off into town on a dusty road to buy red velvet for Katryn's Christmas ball gown.

"Where is the buggy when you need it most?" Katryn asked.

"At the blacksmith's getting a new wooden wheel," Lizbeth answered. "Your five trunks proved too heavy considering the weight of nine more people."

"Where's Timothy when you need him?" Katryn chuckled. "How is your brother anyway?" she asked with a smile. "He stopped writing to me after he graduated from Columbia Law and married a New York socialite with money. Oh yes, don't tell me; he is practicing law and moonlighting as a pig farmer in Lancaster, right?"

"Right! How did you know?" Lizbeth responded.

"Just did," Katryn remarked. "He was always hardworking and determined to succeed."

Brigham's general store did carry the red velvet needed to make Katryn's gown, and Lizbeth designed it from a picture she found in a Montgomery Ward catalog and finished sewing it three hours before the ball commenced. Talk about stress!

The moment of truth came for Katryn. The cold air hit her pink cheeks as she emerged from the four-horse-drawn buggy with her blonde tresses piled high on her majestic head and her diamond earrings dangling. There was a small diamond tiara set above her bangs. She wore a black velvet cape with red satin lining and a red velvet gown accompanied by high white cotton gloves and black velvet shoes. Katryn was more than ready to meet her Prince Charming, Thomas Michael Huntzmon. Poor unsuspecting cowboy, he didn't have a chance.

The Christmas Ball

The Christmas ball was well attended, with ladies and gentlemen dancing as Katryn and the Bozemons entered the ballroom. There were four tables covered with cups of punch and trays of sweet hors d'oeuvres. Christmas wreaths tied with red velvet bows hung on the windowsills with a bright candle shining out into the dark streets, and fresh green fir garland scalloped the walls, which caused the room to smell like Christmas.

Once the women had entered the ballroom, a bell clanged. They were announced by Bishop Dunn. All heads turned toward the beautiful blonde princess in the red velvet gown. Katryn had beads of sweat on her forehead, wondering if Thomas was looking at her. But she knew a proper woman should never appear anxious and desperate for a man. Her strategy was to dance with everyone who asked her—and plenty of young men had signed her dance card and inquired of Martin who this exquisite, delicate creature was. Katryn looked but failed to see Thomas Huntzmon's name anywhere on her card. She started to worry that he wouldn't ever see her at her finest. *Oh dear, suppose his little daughter is ill? She thought I wouldn't be able to blame him for not attending.* But then, just as Katryn was about to give up hope of meeting Thomas, a tall, buffed gentleman dressed in a black tuxedo strutted into the ballroom. He had curly blond hair and piercing blue eyes. He was very handsome. Her heart began to flutter like a monarch butterfly jumping off a rosebush. Her eyes met his. He smiled and felt his knees weaken. Then he turned around. Like a turtle, he wanted to retreat to a safer place to catch his breath and ponder his next move since he had just encountered the most beautiful woman he'd ever seen—and wearing his favorite color. Her Greek-sculpted face was fascinating, and her body was voluptuous and elegant in a ladylike way. His heart told him he wanted her, his loins desired to make love to her, and God told him she would become wife number three. *Be patient!*

Meanwhile, Katryn was in shock; she could feel her knees give out. She braced herself and then felt her body touch the floor. She twisted her right ankle. When her embarrassed red face looked up, her Prince Charming was gone. Katryn wanted to cry, but her ladylike manners prevented her from appearing as a young child. Besides, what would her father say after he'd taught her never to show her emotions in public? Her ankle was killing her with throbbing pain.

CHAPTER 7
THE RECOVERY / LEG OF LAMB

The next six weeks seemed endless to Katryn. *Thank heavens that Martin knew how to make crutches from the extra lumber he was saving in the barn,* she thought. Katryn was still asking herself if her clumsiness scared Thomas Huntzmon away for good. *Of course not!* she reassured herself as she stared in the bedroom mirror. *He wouldn't dare reject this perfect specimen of beauty and culture. After all, I can play Mozart and Beethoven on the piano blindfolded, make blueberry crepes, and bake the best cherry tarts in Utah Territory. He wouldn't dare reject such a fine cook. Or would he? Oh, he won't be able to resist my long blonde hair, these baby-blue eyes, a coveted turned-up nose, and my perfectly smooth radiant skin. Perhaps he was called away on an emergency at home. I hope his baby daughter is okay,* she said to herself.

Katryn heard Lizbeth's voice on the other side of her bedroom door. "Glory be, Katryn, are you awake? May I come in?"

The bedroom door slowly opened with a squeaky sound. Looking around the room, Lizbeth didn't see her friend, but she did notice the French doors wide open to the balcony, so she walked outside.

"Katryn, what are you doing out here all by yourself and in your nightie?"

"I'm just looking out at the Huntzmon ranch, where my beloved lives. I just can't get his handsome face and beautiful physique out of my pretty head. I just know I will see him again, and I feel it in the pit of my heart."

"Well, a little food will help you get stronger. Here is a tray of hot flapjacks with fresh strawberry jam, some honey, and a couple of soft-boiled eggs and warm buttermilk biscuits with hot cocoa. And stop worrying about Thomas; you two are destined to be together for all eternity."

Katryn continued to stare toward Thomas's ranch and didn't answer Lizbeth.

"Katryn, are you listening to me?"

"Oh, I'm so sorry. I was dazing into the vista, admiring the cactus flowers in bloom; they are just beautiful in the hues of spring flowers—purple, red, yellow, and pink."

"We are certainly experiencing an early spring. Usually, they don't bloom until mid-April," Lizbeth added.

"And a big fat yes to all the delicious food on the tray. I am famished. You sure went into a lot of trouble, but I do appreciate the pampering. I figure two more days, and I will be able to help cook and watch the children," added Katryn.

"But the doctor said you needed two solid weeks off your feet, and I strongly suggest you follow his orders," declared Lizbeth.

"Okay, I'll try honoring the doctor's request. I know what I can do in bed: darn all the socks and ripped aprons. In my early teenage years, I was quite a seamstress. So bring on the work before I go stir-crazy, please!"

"Sounds like a great idea. Martin beats his socks up with his thick pointed toes. I have some dresses that need mending and some aprons too, and the kids keep pulling on them until they tear. So there you have it, lots of work to occupy your idle time," Lizbeth said.

"You think of everything, girlfriend. I feel useful already." Katryn chuckled. "I can mend my aprons and then design my wedding gown."

The days and nights seemed to pass quickly; Katryn didn't have time to think of Thomas. After supper, she would retire and read her

Book of Mormon. She knew without a doubt that becoming a Mormon was the sure way to Thomas's heart. It would be a deal breaker if she didn't join his church. He wanted a righteous wife who would marry him in the temple, be sealed to him for all eternity, and teach his children the gospel. Katryn wanted to become Mrs. Thomas Huntzmon with every cell in her body, so she chose to convert to Mormonism and give up her Jewish faith. *After all,* Katryn thought, *the original Mormons—Nephites, Laminites, and Jaredites—came from Israel and were Jewish. So Mormons are like one of the lost tribes of Israel. I will fit in just fine. Their laws will become mine; their rituals, I will follow; their scriptures, I will read and teach to our children.* And so, she converted.

Leg of Lamb

Katryn looked very cute in her red-and-green-plaid floor-length pinafore and matching hat that Lizbeth had made for her as a present for the forthcoming holidays. While she was busy getting a leg of lamb out of the oven, she heard footsteps entering her domain. Now there were two different voices: one she recognized as Martin's and one she had never encountered. Could it be Thomas? Her stomach fluttered with butterflies, her heart started beating faster, and she was about to dump the roast and hot pan on the floor, thinking she might meet him dressed in rags.

"Let me help you, little darlin'," quipped the cowboy, who was wearing a brown ten-gallon Stetson hat. "Seems too heavy for a delicate woman like yourself."

As Katryn looked up to say thank you, she saw him, the one she'd been dreaming about: blond, dreamy-eyed, and gorgeous in his bright blue shirt and tight-fitting tan pants. Her heart skipped a beat, and his smile made his dimples stand out.

"Thank you, kind sir, but I did not need your assistance. Still, I do appreciate the gesture."

Quick Comeback Sally, I'll call her, thought Thomas. *Why, she is a complete package, beautiful, intelligent, and headstrong. She wouldn't admit to needing help if her life depended upon it—just how I like my wives. Why I'll have her eating right out of the palm of my hand in no time. Got to get her into my marriage bed, that's all. My past two wives submitted to my charms after the wedding night; that curlicue thing I do with my tongue before I put in my diamond stud gets them every time. At one point, they get so tense they scream with endless passion; it hurts my eardrums. But what can I say? I'm the man of their dreams, always ready to, please!* He grinned.

"Dinner was superb!" Thomas said. "You're a mighty fine cook, Miss Katryn. I loved all those fixings with the lamb: corn pudding, milky sweet potatoes, homemade mint jelly, green peas and baby onions in cream sauce, bourbon-fried carrots, sweet cinnamon butter, and yeast rolls. The dessert was even better—apple cherry cobbler and ice cream. A feast if I say so myself!" remarked Thomas. "My compliments to the chef!"

Throughout dinner, Katryn noticed Thomas's hands; they were extremely red and were starting to blister.

"Oh, dear!" Katryn said. "Mr. Huntzmon, your hands are burnt from that no-good pan the lamb was in. You just can't go home like that."

"She's right," Martin said with a grinning smile as he gave his lovely wife, Lizbeth, a slight kick under the table. "Holding onto the reins will tear up your hands while you gallop across the purple sage."

"You may stay in the guest room next to Katryn's and the nursery," replied Lizbeth, kicking her husband harder and fluttering her eyelashes at him.

Mr. Gorgeous stayed for two weeks. He put on a few noticeable pounds around his middle and needed to make an extra notch on his belt. He was so enamored by Miss Katryn's barbecue brisket that he just knew he wanted to spend his entire life with her for time and all eternity.

Katryn was smitten by Thomas's kind heart and his sharp wit. He was going to be hard to handle at first, but she'd get him trained in no time. She sincerely wanted to become Mrs. Thomas Huntzmon, wife number three. It didn't make a difference that Thomas wasn't a virgin like she was. One of them needed to know the ropes, as cowboys say.

During the two weeks, Thomas hung out in the kitchen with Katryn, reading her the entire Book of Mormon and answering all her questions about Joseph Smith and the saints' exodus to Zion. Finally, Thomas had a question for her.

He got down on one knee and asked her to be his wife for now and into eternity, and she said yes. They decided to marry in June. Thomas got up and started to dance with his betrothed around the kitchen.

"What's going on in here?" Lizbeth asked with a big smile.

"We're getting married in June!" Thomas gleefully exclaimed.

"Congratulations are in order, so, Wife, break out the buttermilk and chocolate cake," Martin ordered.

"This day is indeed a very blessed one," said Lizbeth. "I wish you two the very best."

"I have one question, future husband: When do I meet your parents?"

"How about this Saturday evening at my parents' ranch? You and the Bozemons are invited to a beef barbecue—nothing special. My mom makes a great seven-layer raspberry vanilla cake with coconut icing. Her grandmother's recipe from Virginia."

"Can we bring anything, Thomas?" Lizbeth asked as she winked at Katryn over the cake announcement.

Thomas thought a bit, smiled at them, and said, "No, just yourselves and my wife, number three."

Meeting Thomas's Parents

The big day came to meet the Huntzmons. Four days had seemed like an eternity to Katryn as she did some serious thinking in Lizbeth's bedroom.

"Whatcha gonna wear today, roommate, pants or a skirt?" Lizbeth asked.

"You took the thoughts right out of my mind," Katryn remarked.

Katryn whisked her body around and held up a delicate lavender lace dress. "This is the one!" she excitedly said. "I simply look divine in this color. Don't you think so? My grandmother's Victorian laced white boots, gloves, and this large-brim yellow straw hat with a lavender ribbon hanging down the back will match perfectly. God takes care of those who take care of themselves. Don't you agree?"

"You would say that Miss Independent, after moving twenty-five hundred miles away from your parents without blinking an eye," Lizbeth teased.

"Wow, aren't you the little hypocrite! Did you conveniently forget you were the one who begged me to move out here to this magical land of enchantment and meet the one and only Thomas Huntzmon of St. George amid the red stone buttes surrounded by desert sand, purple sage, sago lilies, and—lest we forget—the cacti in bloom with fuchsia, red, yellow, and pink blossoms!" Katryn exclaimed.

"Hey, Princess, let's not tarry over such trivial and mundane facts. Hurry up and dress. I'm famished, and I can smell that barbecued beef from here," Lizbeth shouted. "Martin will drive us while we sit back, enjoy the scenery and plan your wedding."

The shiny black Amish carriage traveled down the road at a moderate speed toward Martin Huntzmon's ranch. In the distance, one could see deer grazing in the beige winter wheat fields. Two tall cedar poles with a crest of a bull with the letter *H* after it greeted them at the ranch's entrance. As the carriage drove under the poles, Katryn felt warm, like she was finally home. There were two large horse pastures surrounded by whitewashed wooden fences on both sides of the loam and gravel driveway. The main house was an orange brick mansion with ten bedrooms, one large nursery, and two kitchens—one on the main floor and the other one in the basement, which were used for canning meats, fish, vegetables, jams, and jellies. Furthermore, the home boasted three bathrooms with white cast-iron bathtubs lined with soft sheets to keep the skin from burning while bathing in bubbles. Also, each room was decorated in gold and silver magnolia-printed wallpaper from New Orleans—Brigham's stores carried only the best merchandise money could buy for his wealthy customers.

"We have arrived at our destination, ladies!" Martin boldly announced. "Please let me assist you down from the carriage, up the stairs, and onto the porch. I insist!" he said.

Miss Esther was there on the front porch, anxious to greet her guests. She glared right into Katryn's beautiful blue eyes and knew God had sent this angel for her son and grandbaby to love and cherish for all eternity. She couldn't help pondering all the beautiful blue-eyed babies Thomas and Katryn would make.

"Welcome to my humble home, everyone. Oh, you must be Katryn, the woman from New York City I've heard so much about. You are gorgeous, cultured, educated, and smartly dressed. My son Thomas has told me so much about his stylish fiancée; he has left nothing out. I love you already, my daughter," Esther said. "Please sit down in the dining room. I will have some cold drinks served to you. Your throats must be very parched after that dusty ride."

"I hope you are ready for the tour of the century, Katryn?" Mama asked. "Tomorrow, Thomas will show you the ranch on horseback."

"I will enjoy that, Mrs. ... I mean Mama," Katryn said after she saw a frown on Esther's face when she attempted to adequately address her as Mrs. Huntzmon. She liked Esther immediately, who made her feel welcome and loved as if she had belonged there for years. Esther was like her: forthright, bold, unpretentious, and trustworthy.

A Native with long brown hair named Brave Eagle took Katryn's and Lizbeth's bags up to their assigned rooms.

"Martin, would you go fetch Thomas? He is out riding on the back forty. We need to have some girl talk," Mama said.

With the three women sitting around the kitchen table, the wedding of a century was planned.

"How many of your family and friends will be attending, dear?" Esther asked Katryn.

"I believe my parents, two brothers, six bridesmaids, several dignitaries from New York's Sacred Four Hundred, and some aristocratic cousins from England and Austria. Mother said to plan for one hundred, but probably only fifty will show," Katryn replied.

"Okay, sixty sounds more plausible for the bride. Now for the groom. We must count all of Thomas's wranglers, some of his Indian church brothers; the Prophet Brigham Young, his favorite wife, Amelia, and his twelve apostles; plus our Bishop Dunn. So, a total of thirty for the groom. We don't want to offend anyone," Mama proclaimed.

"If I may interject," Lizbeth said, "I can get the St. George Women's Relief Society to arrange flowers in the church and make candy tokens wrapped in white voile and tied with a pink ribbon to give out to the guests. In addition, they would love to make some powdered sugar-covered apple strudel, juicy yellowish-brown sauerkraut served over the whitest mashed potatoes, and dark pumpernickel bread to accompany the pork roast."

"My mother will want to design a seven-layer wedding cake with her signature colors—edible silver pearls, pink rosebuds, and white coconut frosting with a sugary bride and groom placed on top," Katryn revealed.

"Sounds delightful and perfect, ladies. I can't wait to meet your mother, Katryn. She sounds like my kind of lady—extremely detailed. Oh! That reminds me. Would you all help me set up the dining room table? I want to use my Staffordshire dishware painted with violets on a pearl-white background from England. They were my great-grandmothers who came over on the *Mayflower*," Esther proudly said.

The women were very impressed and adored Mama's Waterford stemmed glasses. They both simultaneously praised her elegant taste. Mama was a little bit of a show-off. After all, she was from a patrician Southern family, related to George Washington, and knew how to entertain properly.

"Everyone, please look at these delicate lacy white Irish napkins my mother made. Aren't they to die for?" Mama asked.

In unison, each woman nodded her head affirmatively. When they were finished setting the table, a perfect picture of elegance emerged with the finest white linen tablecloth, lacy napkins, a vase of pink long-stem roses from the garden as the centerpiece, and an abundance of fresh vegetables, succulent fruits, roasted pork, sweet butter, and light brown smooth mushroom gravy.

Brave Eagle rang the supper bell, and everyone took their seats where their name tags were placed. Mrs. Huntzmon came from a Virginia family and had acquired the art of entertaining from her mother, who had learned it from her mother, and so forth and so on. Her skills, indeed, were displayed tonight!

Papa said grace: "Heavenly Father, we thank you for all the blessings you have been so generous to bestow upon all of us. Also, thank you for this year's bountiful harvest, our well-being, and our prosperity. Please bless this supper and keep us close to your heart. In the name of our Lord. Amen!"

"Please pass the mashed potatoes and sauerkraut first, then the creamed asparagus. Father will cut the pork roast. Everyone, will you please pass him your plates? The yeast rolls are in green straw baskets on the table, and the delicious sauerkraut is in the pink rosebud bowl. Guten Appetit!" Mama wished.

After the sumptuous dinner, all the guests stood around the

newly polished Baldwin baby grand piano made in 1857 for Grandmother Stevens and later passed down to Mama. It was amazing that the trip from Virginia hadn't scratched it much.

Mama arched her back, raised her head, and started playing briskly. Everyone sang "Amazing Grace" and "Onward, Christian Soldiers," followed by "God Bless America." All had a great time.

Six O'clock the Next Morning

Sunrise came at 6:00 a.m. Thomas met Katryn downstairs in the kitchen as planned. They discovered a picnic basket of cinnamon rolls, grape juice in two glass-covered mugs, and deviled eggs sprinkled with paprika.

"This basket has Mama written all over it," Thomas said.

Soon the happy couple were in the buggy to tour the ranch.

"Darling, I want to take you to my favorite place in the whole world."

"That's a tall order, dear," Katryn replied. "Am I dressed for the occasion?" she asked.

Thomas checked her appearance before he gave his approval of her brown riding britches, camel-colored boots, brown felt hat, and beige tailored blouse with a starched collar that was tucked in her pants under a light brown suede vest.

"You look perfect as usual, darling; your clothing style suits your personality."

"Oh! Just what traits are you referring to, Thomas dear?"

"You know, appropriate, tailored, and elegant," he said after much careful thought.

"Well, my sweetheart, do the birds and bees, rabbits, and deer approve, too?" she asked with a big smile.

Thomas just winked back.

"Here we are, darling, just over that ridge. We will need to walk from here, and I'll carry the picnic basket, and you will carry the blanket. Maybe a ten-minute walk."

Off they went until they found Thomas's lucky spot. Thomas had conceived his first two children here thanks to his fertile German bloodline.

Suddenly a deer peeked out from the oak brush and saw a blanket spread out on the grass with apples, cheese, grapes, and pear juice inside the opened basket. Her tail began to move, and she came closer and nosed a blouse and then a pair of britches away from the basket. Then she saw the two lovebirds making silly motions she didn't recognize. Unbeknown to the betrothed, Mama had spiked the grape juice with red burgundy wine, hoping for a grandson, something everyone did in the Old Country when a son was desired.

"We'd better get back, darling. It's getting dark, and we can't miss supper. Papa gets very insulted when I miss Mama's creations. Tonight, is goulash night with homemade egg noodles and delicious tender stew meat in rich brown gravy with fresh peas, yeast rolls, and butter. Cherry pie and vanilla bean ice cream is for dessert."

As the happy, satisfied, and confident couple walked into the house, Mama took one look at the red spot on the back of Katryn's riding skirt and then asked if an early summer wedding would work for her. Katryn wasn't sure, but Mama said, "I insist! Trust me! Expediency is of the essence here! Time passes quickly when you are having fun, Katryn."

Oh my, Katryn thought to herself, *Mama knows!*

CHAPTER 8
THE WEDDING OF THE CENTURY

Despite Katryn's parents' spending ten thousand dollars on a wedding dress from Paris, attaching the Wellington railroad car to the Union Pacific, paying for all the bridesmaids' train tickets and gowns, and preparing for two barbecue beefs on a spit with oodles of roasted corn and baked potatoes, thirty pounds of asparagus from the burnt ditches of the Huntzmons' ranch, and a four-foot-high vanilla and chocolate wedding cake with five pounds of icing, the train was delayed in Omaha, Nebraska, because of inclement weather—bad summer storms that brought down trees, boulders, and run-down miners' shacks. What a mess and a disappointment for the passengers.

"Duke, isn't there anything that can be done?" asked Katryn's mother, Frenchie.

"I am afraid there is no way we are making the wedding today or the next week; the conductor told me. I am so sorry, darling. As we speak, he is sending a telegraph to Salt Lake, which will reach Katryn and Thomas tomorrow. So, we might as well remain calm and play some bridge."

"Does anyone have a deck of cards?" Duke asked.

"Are you kidding? We sorority girls who live on bridge bet you a six-point spread," replied Annie, one of Katryn's bridesmaids.

"You're on," said the Duke of Wellington. "Come over here and sit down and have a drink with me, darling. You will bring me some luck."

"I am sorry, but I can't think straight right now. My baby girl is getting married without her father and me. How dreadful. Katryn must be all shaken up. That's all she talked about when she was a child of ten, her perfect wedding, and how she would wear my gown and walk down the aisle with her proud papa by her side.

"Duke, you're right. I do need a drink! Move over. I'm feeling lucky!"

The telegraph they sent, dated June 8, 1871, read as follows:

Darling Katryn and Thomas. Stop.
Storm has prevented our arrival. Stop.
Returning to New York. Stop.
Carry on with our loving spirits. Stop.
Make some grandchildren. Stop.
Mom and Dad. Stop.

In St. George Temple in southern Utah, in the city of St. George, Bishop Dunn officiated the Huntzmon–Wellington wedding as the happy couple knelt before God on opposite sides of each other, facing an altar of red and white roses. Afterward, Bishop Dunn asked the couple to recite the vows they wrote after they had recited the traditional vows.

Katryn went first. "Thomas Huntzmon, from the first time I saw you, I fell for you, literally, even though you didn't notice me. Thank God! I remember how handsome you looked in your black suit, bright white shirt, and shiny silver buckle. I couldn't see the color of your eyes; nevertheless, I knew they were piercing blue because they touched my heart. Tears fell from my wistful eyes. But why I fell in love with you, chéri, was that simple spark of humility I found when I looked into your soul during the time I nursed you at Lizbeth's. I am here today to take you as my husband as you take me for your wife. May we have a bountiful and prosperous litter of forget-me-nots, so precious and beautiful in God's eyes and ours that they will become missionaries and good Mormons. Also, I will be faithful, loving, and patient but not quiet; I will speak my mind and expect you to do the same. And, Thomas Huntzmon, you will always have my heart. Amen!"

Thomas followed up with his vows: "Katryn Wellington, the first time I ever saw you was at the Christmas ball for just a New York second. Your fair beauty hypnotized me and frightened me at the same time. You took my breath away; I had to leave the room and compose myself. I found myself leaving and running away from the one person I was destined to meet, love, and grow old with. Fat chance I was ever going to escape you. It was destiny how we met: in a kitchen where you needed my help. And you never stopped asking, and I hope you never will, regardless of your independent spirit, which is one of the reasons I am so crazy about you. Also, my precious Katryn, I promise to love you forever and into eternity and hold your hand during all our children's births. I also will be faithful, loving, and patient and will definitely share my thoughts. And, Katryn, you will always have my bleeding heart. Amen!"

The happy couple left the temple sealing room and proceeded to the grand reception at the Huntzmon ranch, which now had access to railroad tracks and a private train that transported the wedding party and guests for the twenty-minute ride. Everyone was jovial and singing and wishing the bride and groom much happiness. Violins were playing songs of Mozart, and children were dancing in the aisles. It was a wonderful time in the land of enchantment!

Arriving at last at their destination, the bride and groom disembarked first and then graciously greeted their guests. The violins continued playing Mozart as all the guests exited the train and walked into a huge white canvas tent decorated with red and white long-stem roses and little baskets of fruit with small sachet bags filled with lavender at each table. Suddenly Martin Bozemon asked for absolute silence from the guests.

"Ladies and gentlemen and children, may I have your attention, please? I would like to introduce Mr. and Mrs. Thomas Huntzmon. They will share their first dance as a married couple with us," he announced as the fiddlers started to play.

Thomas grabbed his bride's hand and kissed her, and everyone roared and whistled. Then he danced the Viennese waltz. Katryn's wedding gown rustled as she dipped, twirled, and pranced around the room. Esther's navy-blue and pink Scottish Tartan plaid wedding dress made of silk taffeta with lace trim, long-fitted mutton sleeves, a V-waisted full skirt, and a white cotton petticoat and stockings and black velvet shoes with silver buckles looked like it all was perfectly made for Katryn.

The bride's blonde hair was piled high upon her head, with ringlets cascading down her face and back and garnished with baby rosebuds. Katryn made a beautiful bride. Too bad her parents were detained in a snowstorm. They would have been proud of her outfit—very European, elegant, and demure, not outlandishly bold in bright pink.

Her blushing husband wore his father's white starched shirt with long sleeves, a gray vest, black pants, and a black suit coat that went down to his knees. His grandfather's gold watch was hanging from his vest pocket—a very handsome gentleman indeed!

The violins started to play soft music and then eased into some favorite Mormon country songs. After five minutes, everyone joined in and had a great time dancing the Virginia reel, the Cotton Eye Joe, the Viennese waltz, and square dancing. Mormons were great dancers.

The food was fantastic, and the punch had been secretly spiked with rum by some teenage pranksters who had to whitewash fences for the entire summer. Happy to say there were many babies born nine months from this wedding date, including one to the lucky bride and groom. The Huntzmons had a boy, 9 lb., 10 oz., and he was named Thomas Huntzmon III. Martin and Lizbeth had a baby girl, 6 lb., 7 oz., and her name was Katrina. The couples had already decided to marry them off to each other when they came of age, but not if they took after their parents, who were stubborn, independent, and idealistic. No one would be telling these future leaders of Mormon society whom to marry.

CHAPTER 9
THE BIG NIGHT

Katryn and Thomas danced their last dance while everyone toasted to their future. The music stopped, and with beautiful fragrant gardenias in her smooth hands, Mrs. Huntzmon turned her back to all the single women and threw her bouquet over her head. The lucky woman to be married next was a tall, stately blonde Norwegian beauty named Elsa Swenson, Thomas's cousin on his mother's side.

The clock struck twelve midnight, and Thomas Martin Huntzmon swept his wife off her feet and carried her up the lighted path to their wedding cottage, where a big surprise awaited them. He kicked the door open and gently placed his wife on the brass bed on top of a white wedding quilt with many colors grouped in sweeping circles made by the St. George Relief Society women. It had many family members' and friends' signatures on a pattern of colorful circles and squares. Indeed, it was a family heirloom that would be passed down through many generations of Huntzmons.

Sweating like a peach, the nervous husband unbuttoned his wife's wedding gown, slipped it off, and let it fall to the hardwood floor. Then he removed her one-piece Mormon undergarment by unraveling the red ribbons. Katryn was now naked and available for Thomas's pleasure. Thomas moved closer to his wife and whispered in her ear what he wanted to do to her.

"You are truly a sensuous, beautiful, God-fearing woman whose creamy breasts with rosebud nipples suck the life out of my loins."

With that said, he mounted her with gentle thrusts until she moaned with screams and sighs of passion. Thomas lay beside this gorgeous woman, his wife until she stopped begging for more. As she lay on her back with satisfaction on her face, Thomas worked his tongue slowly and passionately around her nipples and sucked them till they hardened. Going downward toward her womanhood, he licked her hard with his tongue. Katryn became aroused and begged him to keep going. He obliged her. Bingo. He hit the spot, and all celestial heaven erupted; her sensuous earthquake came.

Thomas and his beloved Katryn slept until noon. When they arose, they bathed in the nearby brook, ate breakfast, dressed, and went for a run into the forest and up a hill until they came to a waterfall.

"My dad took my mother here on their wedding night, and they found this waterfall. They went behind it and found a cave where someone had built a fire. Probably one of the Indian tribes took refuge here during hunting season. Also, there is a pond where my father and mother conceived me. So I thought we might try to conceive a baby there. It appears to be a lucky spot."

"Sounds like a plan; let's do it," Katryn agreed.
Off the newlyweds went in search of adventure. Th
ey walked up the hill to Deer Pond, where they undressed, dove into the cool water, swam, and played water tag. Then Katryn suggested they go behind the waterfall and follow Huntzmon tradition. Off they went like two wild deer, with Thomas following Katryn's scent. *Splash!*

CHAPTER 10
THE HONEYMOON

The late 1860s was a period in history when air travel had not yet been invented. However, the horseless iron carriage became a reality once the Baltimore and Ohio Railroad took its maiden voyage in 1830. A very ingenious California gentleman named Asa Whitney had gotten rich trading with the Far East. But there was a tiny downside: No railroad tracks connected the Pacific and the Atlantic Oceans. After returning from a trip to China, he realized this need. So Asa set out to promote his dream by writing articles describing the benefits of using a train to transport goods and people across the country in four days and also participating in international trade with China and Japan. He and Abraham Lincoln knew this big step would make the United States of America the world's greatest and most powerful nation.

On April 6, 1869, Asa's dream was achieved. The First Transcontinental Railroad emerged with that last golden spike at Promontory Point outside of Ogden, Utah. President Lincoln was a huge supporter of Asa's project and led Congress to give money in the form of government bonds and free tracts of land to the Union Pacific to help build the first transcontinental railroad. Thus, the United States was now a force to compete with in foreign markets, helping it become one of the wealthiest nations in the world.

While the United States government financed the Union Pacific in the East, four industrious men financed the western portion of this project: Leland Stanford, Charles Crocker, Collis Huntington, and Mark Hopkins. Their enterprise was called the California Pacific Railroad.

"And that, my pretty wife, is how the West was really won," explained Thomas. "Furthermore, Leland is distant kin on his great-grandmother Julia's side, who is a second cousin to my grandfather John Joseph."

"Is he a Mormon, too?" asked Katryn.

"No, but there is hope. The church has many missionaries in Sacramento, so he is sure to hear the scriptures from them. I also hear that Leland has a huge farm somewhere out west where he raises horses and grows many fruits and vegetables, then sells them resale to the US Army and makes a fortune."

"Sounds like a place we can visit when we're out there on our honeymoon, darling," Katryn exclaimed with a romantic gaze.

"Whatever you desire, my love. I adore you and am excited to show you my favorite places in California, which I visited with my father when I was a young boy. Places such as Potter's Gold Mine, Fort Reno, Strawberry Creek—where we fished—and the San Francisco Bay and the Pacific Ocean, where we sailed and swam for hours."

"Thomas, I really would love to see all those places. I can't wait."

"You won't have to wait, my darling; we leave on the Union Pacific from Salt Lake in two days."

"Oh my gosh!" Katryn jumped up and down. "What shall I pack? I must bring warm clothes for those high Sierras and a woolen sweater for those cool breezes from the Pacific Ocean. I need boots as well as comfortable shoes. Also, many dresses and a gown for the San Francisco Black and White Ball, plenty of frilly petticoats and lingerie, white knitted socks, and church garments with side ribbons. Oh! And those galoshes and an umbrella, just in case it rains in San Francisco. Thomas, I plan to be the best, most elegantly dressed woman west of Salt Lake. I am going to make you very proud of the way I look. After all, my husband is the richest cattle baron in the Utah Territory."

Thomas just chuckled as he thought of all the money, he would be spending at Brigham's Emporium to support such a celebrity wife of this cattle baron.

On a beautiful, sunny, brisk June day, the conductor yelled, "All aboard." Monday morning, the cattle baron, his wife, and the Union Pacific Railroad left the Salt Lake station as scheduled, precisely at 8:00. There were no time zones at this time. The Huntzmons had a leisurely brunch in their private railroad car and rested as newlyweds did after a couple of sensuous romps in bed, on the table, and in the Victorian bathtub.

Gambling Scene on the Train

"Darling, what shall I wear to supper tonight? It's a very special occasion for us, so I must wear something spectacular that reeks of greenbacks. It's our one-week anniversary, and the Clarks and Fletchers want to celebrate with us by holding an intimate dinner party in our honor."

"Yes, but after dinner, we men are going to retire in the Oxford Room to chitchat about President Grant and his policies' effects on our economy."

"Boring! Money and politics, politics and money; that's all you men ever think about," shouted Katryn with a big sour grin.

"And just what do women talk about?" asked Thomas, chuckling out loud.

"Current events, fashion, and the latest gossip—and in that order. After all, darling, these ladies are affluent, cultured, and Protestant and belong to long lines of blue bloods like my father, the duke.

"But if these ladies were Mormon, we would be discussing our scriptures, recipes, child-rearing, and Relief Society news. And we just might play bridge," she added. "Protestant ladies do not have the market on playing bridge, and Mormon ladies have been known to beat them."

"Honey, do you even know how to play? That game is for smart people." He pompously laughed, showing a big, handsome, boyish smile.

"Thomas Huntzmon, you are incorrigible!" she cried out. "I'll have you know your brainy wife was the champion bridge player at the East Hampton Episcopalian Ladies Club in New York three years in a row."

With a smile and in a New York second, Thomas was gone—vanished. *Men,* she thought, *are so predictable.* Katryn just shook her pretty head with an upsweep of blonde curls twinkling about with diamond barrettes, then continued primping. She applied medium-pink lipstick to her plump heart-shaped lips and brushed matching rouge on her high cheekbones. Next, she put on the breast corset to lift her firm, creamy breasts and treat Thomas to a tingling sensation down under. Second, to last on the list, Katryn squeezed into pink satin pumps that laced up the middle. Last, she slipped a pink silk gown over her head. *Voilà! Ready to go! Oops, no Mormon garments this evening. They will only be chucked to the floor later on, anyway. I hate inefficiency,* she thought.

The breathtaking Mrs. Thomas Huntzmon entered the private dining car abandoned but exquisitely dressed in the latest shimmering light pink silk gown from Paris. Katryn walked into the dining car with a breath of confidence and an air of graciousness and humility—something she had learned from the many Mormon families who had lost everything more than twice as they made their way to Zion. She had read about them in the *Nauvoo Daily Newspaper* that Lizbeth gave her. No matter what happened to these women, they just shrugged it off and kept going.

"Good evening, ladies. You all look amazing," Katryn exclaimed.

"You look amazing yourself. Simply Parisienne, my dear," Marcia Clark said.

The rest of the women were very complimentary with colorful adjectives about Katryn's shimmering pink gown and matching shoes. They appreciated style and elegance, and Katryn had it all.

Plus, she had a wealthy stud for a husband, which made her women friends envious. Most of their husbands were past their prime. Molly Fletcher loved Katryn's flawless makeup and asked, "Where did you purchase your makeup, dear?"

Katryn responded, "Macy's in New York City, where they carry the latest French fashions and products like Estée Lauder. I have them mail me what I want from their catalog. It comes on the train. I heard a rumor from my mother that Macy's is heading to Salt Lake and will be located right on Main Street. She knows the owner, Isidor Straus. Goods will be shipped to Ogden and then onto Salt Lake. Get this, ladies: If your dress doesn't fit properly, you can ship it back on the train, and the correct item will be sent to you approximately four days later after alterations. Isn't that a delicious idea?" Katryn asked. They unanimously agreed by clapping their hands.

"Remember, ladies. It is just a rumor." Katryn chuckled. "Maybe instead of a Brigham Young's department store chain called ZMCI, a Macy's will magically appear. Only time will tell."

"But why a store in Salt Lake?" inquisitive Marcia just had to ask.

"Good question! The location of a department store was a gift from the Union Pacific, a gesture to say thank you to the Mormons who worked tirelessly laying tracks and digging holes for telegraph poles until the golden spike was placed in the track that connected the Union and California Pacific Railroads, making them into one big transcontinental railway at Promontory Point in Ogden, Utah, on May 10, 1869."

Sharon exclaimed, "I am so impressed. You and your husband are the only Mormons we know."

"Same here, and you're fun and interesting," Marcia added. "Here," she said as she lifted her champagne glass with bubbly in it, "I would like to make a toast to the Mormons. Hip, hip, hooray to the Utah pioneers who were responsible for this train we are on. We are all going to San Francisco, and we couldn't have done it without that golden spike put in by those glorious hardworking, and dedicated souls in Ogden, Utah. May they prosper and multiply! To the Mormons, hip, hip, hooray!"

They all drank and partied through the evening. Katryn sang church hymns with Marcia and Molly. Katryn always sipped real grape juice when her lips were dry. The maid walked in and heard them singing "Amazing Grace." On her way to put more Chablis in everyone's glass, her little body swayed to the music. Her name was Pauline, and she and her husband worked the trains on weekends. They had a large family of five children and needed money for their education. Coloreds really valued a strong Christian education for their children, who were second-generation Americans. Pauline and her husband eventually educated all five and produced one doctor, one lawyer, one nurse, and one college professor from Dartmouth. The youngest, Clarence, became a minister of the First Methodist Church of Atlanta. Martin Luther King Jr. was his great-grandson.

In the Oxford Car Playing Cards

There was a player piano, and all the men were gathered around singing. JJ Fletcher was hitting the keys, Oli Clark was singing baritone, and Thomas was whistling to the tune of "America the Beautiful." Surprisingly, a bottle of Chablis was half full on the table with three empty glasses, and Thomas's glass was still full.

What a surprise the Huntzmons had in store for them when they returned to their room! They both ordered a bottle of bubbly cider for a nightcap, along with milk chocolates. They were both feeling very amorous. Neither one drank, so they just spent a couple of hours in a boring situation except for the singing.

Katryn returned to their railroad car first. The brass bed was turned down with a small gold-wrapped chocolate mint on each white silk pillowcase. There were fresh-cut red roses on the dresser, and the room was filled with their sweet aroma. Quickly, Kathryn slipped out of her gown and corset and jumped into bed, leaving her clothing on the floor, including her Mormon garments. Katryn still smelled like flowers. Earlier, she had sprayed herself from head to toe with the French lavender cologne Anjou No. 3.

Suddenly the door opened, and a very confused man wobbled into the bedroom. He fell over the Queen Anne chair and then vomited all over the English bathroom.

"Is that you, Thomas?" she asked.

"Who else, my sweet? I ate something rotten that made me puke. I'll clean up and sleep on the couch, so you are protected from this odor. By the way, honey, where is your perfume? I need to spray."

Katryn put her head under her pillow as she pointed to her French cologne. She wished she were elsewhere, like in her rose garden on the ranch.

Morning came too soon for Thomas. He opened his baby blues when the porter, Pauline's husband, Von, knocked on the door then entered with a silver tray of steaming hot chocolate, soft-boiled eggs, steaks, buttermilk biscuits, strawberry jam, and freshly squeezed orange juice. He saw that the newlyweds were not up yet, so he just placed everything on the oak table and left, shaking his head and laughing at such weaklings. *What is this world coming to?* he thought. *These young folks just have to learn to hold their liquor.*

CHAPTER 11
THE PALACE HOTEL

The Union Pacific pulled into the San Francisco station on time at 12:00 noon. The weather was balmy, about sixty-seven degrees, and you could smell the hyacinths in the air. There were also red, white, and pink tulips, daffodils, and cherry blossoms everywhere you looked. In addition, San Francisco had unique weather and the ambiance of a paradoxical society: Nob Hill with its wealthy elite—aristocrats, railroad tycoons, European royalty—and the Barbary Coast flush with miners, brothels, entrepreneurs, and opportunists.

The Huntzmons were elegantly escorted to the Palace Hotel in a four-horse-drawn carriage. Katryn had brought so much Louis Vuitton luggage that she and Thomas could barely squeeze into their seats.

"Perhaps you would prefer to sit on top with the driver, my pretty darling?"

"Now, Thomas, you are toying with me. There is no top, just fresh air. I do love these red leather seats. They are pretty to look at and smooth to touch. We should get some for our carriages. Black is passé and impractical—it collects a great deal of dirt. Oh! Look, Thomas, at that huge building in front of us. It takes up the entire block between New Montgomery and Market Streets. Wait, I am counting, and it's seven stories tall. Wow! Just like the Grand Hotel in Paris! What did you say, Thomas? Sorry, I wasn't listening. Can you blame me with all this splendor?"

"What did you expect, Katryn? It's San Francisco, the fastest-growing city in California. And I have a surprise for you, darling!"

"What is it, dear?"

"That huge building you are so enamored with is our hotel for the week, and I hear the inside is spectacular. And we are on the top floor in the Honeymoon Suite facing San Francisco Bay," Thomas announced.

"The brochure advertises, Thomas, that we can look upon the entire city at night and see a beautiful array of colorful jewels: thousands of sparkly diamonds in the sky and bright rubies and emeralds throughout the city. And in the daytime, we can see the wharf and San Francisco Bay filled with sailboats and steamers," Katryn added.

The horses took a right turn and followed a driveway that led up to a circular building with a multicolored stained-glass roof. Once parked in front of the main door, the bride and groom exited and went through the huge mahogany doors. The concierge and bellboy met them at the door and escorted Mr. and Mrs. Huntzmon up to their suite. Later, Katryn would tell Mama that they did not have to climb stairs. "We took something called an elevator, which works by using gravity. One thing goes up while another goes down. Simple physics, they say."

"We were wondering, who picks up the horses' poop, Albert, the industrious bellboy? The entranceway was very clean today," Katryn said.

"You will never see horse poop here at the Palace Hotel. Several young boys are paid to keep a watchful vigil 24/7."

As Katryn and Thomas walked into the lobby, they couldn't believe what they saw. Beautiful landscape paintings by Renoir and French mirrors trimmed in gold leaf were hung on all four walls, palm trees were scattered in the lobby, and six bouquets of fresh-cut roses of all colors were on the front desk. The skylight had multicolored stained-glass squares and triangles. The dark-stained wall panels were made of strong oak from the hotel's private forest. The bar had a huge rectangular painting of the Pied Piper, which still hangs there today.

"I feel just like royalty, Thomas. My arms have goosebumps all over, and my taste buds are requesting sugar and honey. I need a sweet fix."

"Well, my darling wife, you are in luck; it is time for afternoon tea! Let's go."

It took five minutes for the elevator to open its doors. The happy newlyweds headed for the silver tea set and sweet pastries. "Looks like they are serving over to that side of the room near the veranda, darling. And guess what? There are cute little tables to sit at," Thomas said. "There, that looks like a good table by the fishpond."

Katryn looked up to the stained-glass ceiling with rich, bold colors of red, yellow, blue, and green and was in awe of the architect, who just happened to be an old friend of hers from New York. In fact, she used to date him. But Katryn had no idea he designed this hotel and now lived in San Francisco.

The waiter brought them mint tea, decadent chocolate cake, a dollop of fresh whipped cream, and a couple of petits fours.

"Is your sweet tooth satisfied, my darling?"

"Yes, my sugar craving has subsided. And yours? Has it been satisfied, Thomas?"

"Not quite. I need more sugar, but I can get that in our boudoir," remarked Thomas.

Off the happy couple dashed out of the bar, and they took an elevator to their honeymoon suite. While carrying his beautiful bride in his arms, Thomas opened the door and said, "Let's see who can crawl under the sheets first—naked, of course!"

With that prompt, Katryn ran fast, stripping her body of her dress and slips, pantaloons, and undergarments and then taking off her shoes. She crawled into bed, and to her surprise, Thomas was already there.

"Not fair!" she cried out. "You don't have as many clothes as I do to remove."

"I'm sorry, precious, but I am hard to beat in a race. I have longer legs than you."

Thomas looked into his wife's blue eyes and just melted. He kissed her with passion, and she reciprocated. Two hours later, they emerged and decided to take a walk in the garden. Before they left, someone knocked at their door. It was a bellboy with an invitation for the happy couple to dine with Mr. Ralston, the owner of the hotel, and a few of his friends. The card read, please be prompt. "Dinner is at eight sharp in the Presidential Suite. Formal attire is required!"

Thomas and Katryn scrambled to find suitable attire. They bathed, dressed, and then dashed down the hall and around the corner to the Presidential Suite, arriving precisely at eight. They could hear laughter inside and couldn't wait for the butler to answer the doorbell. It seemed like an hour until the door opened, but it was only a few seconds. Their anticipation of meeting Ralston was very high. The room was filled with around twenty couples, and all were decked out in fashionable formal attire. They were the cream of San Francisco's Society who lived on Nob Hill. The host greeted them at the door and led them inside.

There were tables filled with red, white, and pink begonias; platters of Chinese shrimp egg rolls; twice-cooked pork; moo goo gai pan; steamed and fried rice; General Tso's chicken, barbecue pork spare ribs, shrimp and scallops lo mein, and spicy red pepper steak; and a tray of stuffed salmon with creamy cucumber sauce surrounded by crab-stuffed tomatoes and mushrooms. Mouthwatering desserts were on a silver cart: chocolate cream puffs, almond cookies, bread pudding laced with buttered rum, Southern coconut cake, strawberry cream tarts, and plenty of sliced fresh fruit topped with whipped cream.

"The dinner is superb!" yelled one of the guests, who was staring at Katryn. He was very handsome with jet-black curly hair—possibly Italian, but his last name was Gordon. Katryn remembered him from her summers at Southampton. He was a good dancer, a sweet and charming flirt, and the late Count Koski's grandson who had proposed to her before going to South Africa to fight in the Boer War. John Gordon had given her a heart-shaped engagement ring with two tiny diamond baguettes on each side of the central diamond. After she thought he had died in the war, she buried the ring in her jewelry chest, locked the chest, and then buried it in her backyard under a lilac tree where they used to sit, hold hands, and talk about their future.

His "missing in action" status and the report of his death—everyone on the train to Zimbabwe was burned to ashes after the rebels blew up the train—contributed to her advancement to move West. Katryn didn't know John had lived because he was thrown far enough into the bushes that the flames didn't reach him. His apparent ill-fated death was devastating to Katryn, so all it took was that timely letter from Lizbeth, and off she went following her dreams of marrying the one.

"Mr. Ralston," Thomas said, "I am so pleased to meet a man with your vision. Your hotel is superb, and I love the huge skylight with the beautiful multicolored stained glass."

Mr. Ralston smiled. "I always love to hear that my hotel pleases my guests. I spent a great deal of time planning the details of that stained glass with my architect, Mr. Garner. He traveled throughout Europe to bring back sketches of the most famous grand hotels in Europe. By the way, would you and your pretty wife care to meet him? He comes from New York as your wife does, Thomas."

"We would love to meet such a talent from New York," Katryn exclaimed in a high-pitched voice, knowing all the time that she had been keeping a huge secret from Thomas.

Just as they were about to meet the architect, they heard a bell and a strong baritone voice.

The Encounter

"Dinner is being served in the adjoining dining room!" stated the tall, slender, silver-haired butler. Everyone ambled to find their name tags on the place mats except the Huntzmons, Mr. Ralston, and Mr. Gordon.

"John, may I present Mr. and Mrs. Huntzmon from the Utah Territory. They are staying in the Honeymoon Suite."

"Pleased to meet you both. Your wife is charming, Mr. Huntzmon. I do believe we know each other from New York. In fact, I proposed to her once, but she turned me down for some pipe dream of finding a righteous man out west." Thomas's face turned red. "None of us Easterners were good enough for her. And I gather she has met 'the one,' as she put it."

"John, I am standing right here in front of your snobbish nose. I hate it when no one talks to me directly." Katryn's cheeks were bright red, so she took three deep breaths. "Your hotel is beautiful and must be your best work yet. The Italian furniture, French drapes, palm trees, gold trim throughout, and amazing stained glass on the lobby's ceiling is superb! Looks very European to me," she was able to report calmly.

"Perhaps you would allow me to show you and your husband the gardens? They are designed after the gardens of Versailles."

"We would love to," replied Thomas, "but another time."

Katryn gently refused John's request after dinner since Thomas had excused himself to join Mr. Ralston in his library to discuss the steak business. She felt uneasy. Her knees felt like they were going to bend, and she felt faint. Seeing her former betrothed, whom she thought was dead, was a massive shock to her. The experience of loving John, then losing him and seeing him alive again—just when she had married someone else—was shocking, shameful, and bittersweet. All Katryn wanted was to retreat to her hotel room and cry. *How did John know all that about my dreams? I bet it was my mother. She never could keep a secret!* Promptly after dinner and politely excusing herself, our heroine retired to her room with a headache. She sat on her bed and stared at that heart-shaped red ruby with diamonds sparkling on her right pinky, which she'd exhumed before she left New York, and cried herself to sleep, only to be awakened in the morning by her husband's gentle kiss on her forehead.

"Thomas, did you change my clothes and put me under the covers?"

"Of course, my darling. And I seemed to have awakened a few of your rosebuds in the process."

Katryn blushed as Thomas kissed her lips and caressed her breasts. They stayed in bed most of the day. Afternoon tea was served in their room on a large sterling silver platter in a Prince Albert china tea set with an accompanying three-tier tray filled with an assortment of petite chocolate raspberry finger cakes and cucumber sandwiches—a feast for a princess like Marie Antoinette, who everyone knows adored cake. In fact, Marie Antoinette was a distant cousin of Katryn's father, the Duke of Wellington.

Following tea, Katryn took a hot vanilla bean and milk bubble bath, which smelled amazing. Thomas watched her slowly slip into the Victorian bathtub, covering her creamy, luscious breasts and succulent nipples with ivory bubbles. *Should I or shouldn't I?* Thomas thought. He took a deep breath, conquered his desires, left the room, took a cold shower in the master bathroom, then dressed.

Evening came soon enough for the Huntzmons, who were famished after a marathon of lovemaking. Katryn looked fabulous— an innocent cherub in a white silk Redfield skirt and fitted jacket, the rage in England and Paris in 1876.

The Palace Hotel was strategically decorated simply but elegantly everywhere. On windowsills, tables, marble stairs, narrow brick paths leading to the garden from the entryway and the front desk, and in each hotel room were vases of colorful flowers—white gardenias, pink, yellow, and crimson-red long-stem roses, yellow daffodils, and deep-purple violets. The lilac trees were in full bloom in the garden room; the sun shone vividly through the colorful stained glass dome high above the foyer—120 feet, to be precise.

A trio of violinists played Mozart in the dining room, where San Francisco's Sacred One Hundred dined nightly. After dinner, the guests danced the Viennese waltz in the sumptuous oak-paneled ballroom, which boasted four dangling Austrian crystal chandeliers. The women's jewels sparkled and complemented each other: bright rubies, bold green emeralds, royal-blue sapphires, and flawless clear diamonds, all worn on their long delicate necks and all in the same room—a jewel thief's dream—which put a heavenly spin on the crystals that reflected the multicolored rays of a rainbow. The French Champagne was flowing, and the guests were happy. But everything stopped when the Royal Guard announced Katryn and Thomas. There at the entrance to the ballroom stood a prince and princess whom everyone wanted to dance with. The Sacred One Hundred clapped their hands and welcomed them with open arms. They all knew Katryn's parents were members of New York's elite gentry. There were many guests from Europe whom Katryn had met on one of her trips: the Rothschilds of Paris, the Count and Countess of Parma, Italy, and the Duke of Cambridge, England. She danced with them until she was ready to drop. Then, when she was prepared to sit, she felt a tap on her shoulder, and a familiar voice asked if he could have the next waltz. Katryn turned her head and saw it was Thomas with a big grin on his handsome face. Into the night, these two lovebirds danced just with each other—one, two, three, one, two, three …

"Thomas, I'm famished for real food; let's get a snack in the Pied Piper Bar. I hear their oyster stew is simply divine and good for the ovaries," Katryn exclaimed.

Thomas wondered if she were pregnant already because all she had been doing today was craving food—more than she'd eaten in a day back home. *No! It's too soon. But I can only hope!* he thought.

They passed by the hotel's entranceway, where they could see those famous California palm trees next to the white marble columns where the elegant carriages dropped off the guests and their expensive Louis Vuitton luggage. Tiny pets were also welcomed, and Katryn heard some dogs barking as they pranced in regal form with their wagging tails standing upright in front of the guests.

"Look, Thomas, over in the corner, there's a guest with four pug puppies—the breed my father's distant cousin had when she was the infamous spending queen of France. Oh, darling, I always had my heart set on having my own pug and naming it Mops. Please, my chéri, make me happy tonight!"

"If you insist. I am only too obliged to grant you your wish. Leave everything to me, Queen Marie Antoinette!"

"Darling, wait. Ask if Mops comes with her own *niche de chien*."

"Her own what?"

Katryn replied, "A dog carrier. The French are renowned for them. They are constructed from gilded beech and pine, covered with soft blue plush velvet, lined with soft striped blue and green silk, trimmed with shiny copper nailheads, decorated with elaborate neoclassical carved wood motifs of acanthus leaves and Greek keys, and sit off the floor four inches—and usually designed by Claud I. Séné." (FYI, one sold at Sotheby's for $183,300 in 2008.)

As Katryn anxiously awaited for Mops to materialize, a gentleman dressed in a black tuxedo admiring her aristocratic features from afar: her chiseled nose, rosy-pink cheeks, ruby-red lips, golden blonde curls piled on top of her head, and delicate peach complexion. Her breasts were smaller than those of the working girls at the brothels, but they were pert with the nipples pointed and were very inviting to a man. Thomas loved them. Jonathan Gaynor admired them from afar and remembered them as being firm to the touch; he thought his former fiancée Katryn Kline Wellington from the Hamptons was glowing and more beautiful today than when she was his. He hadn't seen her since he left New York to design the Grand Elizabeth Hotel in South Africa prior to the Anglo-Zulu War. He'd attempted to find her many times when he returned, but she had moved out west, which was the reason he had accepted a commission from Ralston to design his family mansion and Palace Hotel in San Francisco, hoping to find her.

Now, at this serendipitous moment, Gaynor was looking at her in a beautiful white silk gown, his heart skipping a beat without her knowledge. This encounter was bittersweet; he felt he could shoot himself. But he would never give up hope of one day making her his queen. *A cowboy's life span is short compared to an architect's,* he thought.

In the meantime, wanting to please his wife, Thomas headed toward the owner of the puppies and successfully completed the purchase for Katryn's new pug, Mops. He took one close look at her and decided she was one scared little skinny pup he would fatten up on corn husks like he did his piglets. *They kind of look alike,* he thought.

Thomas returned with the puppy and her forest-green velvet carrier just as Jonathan started to walk toward Katryn until the latter saw the pup and laughed so hard that he excused himself and headed toward the gentlemen's lounge.

"Oh, Thomas, thank you so much. She is so adorable. Little Lizette will love her too! Mops do not look like one of your piglets; she looks more like a little lamb—helpless, defenseless, and needing lots of love."

"Whatever you say, my darling. You'd better add food to your list. She's mighty hungry, Katryn. Look how she is nibbling at my alligator boots. A young pup needs beef!"

"Yes, my darling," Katryn replied, "I know. Let's order prime rib and give little Mops the bones with an inch of rare beef on each side."

Everyone was watching with amazement as the elegantly dressed couple ate tender, juicy beef sandwiches while their dog devoured their juicy prime rib bones in the elegant Pied Piper Bar. Built in 1875, the Pied Piper attracted many foreign dignitaries and Nob Hill socialites; served American and Continental food; carried the finest beer, wine, and hard liquor; offered excellent service; and hired the best musicians and opera singers in all of San Francisco to entertain its guests.

The atmosphere in the Pied Piper was like that of an English gentlemen's private club boasting cherrywood-paneled walls decorated with gold trim mirrors, hanging Austrian chandeliers, mahogany tables, and green leather-back Queen Anne chairs. It was an ambiance of elegance where guests felt they were treated like royalty.

The most popular feature of the Pied Piper Bar was an original painting, from which the bar acquired its name, by an unknown talented artist hanging on the wall like those naked women paintings in western saloons. It had the same artistic effect—one of rare pleasure for the exotic and sensuous art connoisseur. So, guests watching Mops and looking at the Pied Piper painting had a double treat, both artistic and comedic.

"Well, darling," one patron said to his wife after she gasped while watching this unusual scene, "this is the Wild West with their own ways of doing things, a philosophy of live and let live, where it appears pets have no boundaries. We need to respect their culture, my darling."

Thomas's keen ears heard that comment, and he just chuckled and then smiled at the couple. He also heard the maître d' announce that he had a letter for Mr. Huntzmon. Thomas waved his white glove, and the waiter brought a white linen note marked with the letter R scribbled in gold to his table.

"Darling, it's from Mr. Ralston."

"Please read it. I am anxious to know what it says," Katryn exclaimed.

Dear Mr. and Mrs. Huntzmon,

You are cordially invited for lunch at my home tomorrow, and I will send a carriage for you at eleven. We are going to play tennis and billiards. I will not take no for an answer!

Your host,
Chap Ralston

"Oh well," Thomas said, "we'd better attend, or we will offend our host. I think we should retire, darling; I can't eat another morsel."

"Ditto!"

"And Mops does need a bath," Katryn added. "And I must find my tennis outfit."

The Luncheon

Morning came. Katryn found Thomas asleep on the couch in the living area with a pillow over his head. Mops's big brown eyes peeked out from beneath Thomas's blue woolen blanket and looked adorable.

"Thomas, darling, please wake up. Mops must go for a walk. We also need to get ready for our luncheon with Mr. Ralston. And don't forget to order our free continental breakfast—croissants, strawberry jam, hot lemon and ginger tea, soft-boiled eggs, and thinly sliced Virginia ham. It's not proper to attend a luncheon on an empty stomach and eat like a swine."

"I'm so confused. I don't know which end is up, Katryn. I now have a third party to care for besides us two," exclaimed Thomas.

"Darling, I wanted Mops, so I will do my best to juggle my schedule and take care of her," replied Katryn. "Or, I have a better idea. I'll call the hotel's concierge; he will get someone to walk her. That is part of their job description, Thomas."

"You and your New York ideas, Katryn; I love them. Where have you been all my life?"

"Waiting for you to find me, Mr. Huntzmon."

The hotel driver was ready at 11:30 sharp, and the Huntzmons plus one boarded the black and yellow carriage to the Ralston estate south of San Francisco, overlooking the Pacific Ocean. They arrived precisely at noon. A sumptuous lunch of cold crab, champagne salad, and freshly squeezed and sweetened lemonade with a vanilla cake iced with lemon frosting was served on the back veranda overlooking a Victorian garden—right out of the novel *Jane Eyre*. Mozart's Violin Concerto No. 3 was coming from a big shiny brass horn attached to a box with a crank on one side. The sun was shining, robins were chirping, and many colorful flowers—begonias, geraniums, roses, and tulips—surrounded the brick patio. The guests included Mr. and Mrs. Ralston, Jonathan Gaynor, his guest Portia, and the Huntzmons. Mr. Leland Stanford was in Washington, DC, at a railroad meeting and had sent his apologies.

"How was the drive from the hotel, Katryn?" Mrs. Ralston asked.

"Very relaxing. Your horses move well together; they are in sync, making the ride here very smooth. When I attended finishing school in Pennsylvania, I used to drive a team around my friend Lizbeth's farm. No one thought a girl could do that, but I proved them wrong. I love well-bred horses, and they always behave like gentlemen and listen to your command," Katryn explained.

"Thomas, how are you enjoying the ocean?" asked Mr. Ralston.

"It is different not to see prairies and livestock roaming freely," Thomas answered. "But it is a nice change to look out and see nothing but water and dream of being on a ship going to the Orient. Also, I love those white foaming bubbles that dance up to the sand and tickle my feet. We have large lakes back home, but they don't give you the same possibilities or sensations that an ocean does."

"I have had the same experience as your wife, Thomas, of seeing the two swallowing oceans bordering our great country—the Pacific and the Atlantic. I swam and sailed both. And do you know, everyone, that it only takes three hours to go around San Francisco Bay on a sailboat with four sails? In fact, I am sailing tomorrow at ten. I'd love for you two charming Westerners to join me. You will have something to talk to your grandchildren about. I might even let you sail, Thomas. Going under the Golden Gate Bridge and cruising the San Francisco waterfront is a blast. We can even stop and have lunch, get a closer look at Angel and Antelope Islands, sail through the beautiful Raccoon Strait, and view Sausalito at sunset." *I'll even let you sail as I make love to Katryn down below,* he thought to himself. John still loved her with every cell of his tanned muscled frame. He had never met another woman like her, so smart, adventurous, and caring for others, as well as possessing a beautiful face with an innocent smile.

"Well, you're on! Right, darling? We Huntzmons love challenges!" Katryn bellowed.

"It sounds lovely, Jonathan, but we have to pack and board the train home by noon tomorrow. Next trip out here for sure, promise!" Thomas responded in the nick of time. He didn't want to give Jonathan an edge over him. He had never been on a sailboat, let alone sailed one. When he returned, he would know how to sail, by gosh! He made a plan to ask Katryn's father, the duke, to teach him. He had sailed all along the Eastern United States, England, and Europe.

"You're no fun, Huntzmons, but I'll hold you to your promise. You don't know what you're missing, guys," Jonathan shouted.

"Thomas, I have a proposition for you about purchasing some of your cattle for my restaurants here at the Palace Hotel," Mr. Ralston said. "Every one of my male guests just loves a Black Angus two-inch steak, medium rare and smothered with onions. My dilemma is that California is not yet set up for cattle grazing, and your Utah Territory is perfect with its open grazing fields and the best alfalfa and corn on this side of Kansas City. Texas cattle are too skinny and tough for my clients by the time they travel up here. So, what do you say, forty dollars a hoof delivered by rail?"

"You've got yourself a deal, Ralston. Let's shake on it. Do you need some of my cowboys to help get the cattle settled?" Thomas asked. "In fact, Katryn and I will come out with them and take you up on some sailing lessons, Gaynor."

"Thomas," Ralston proclaimed, "I'll be looking forward to all those steaks on the hoof coming in September. And I will have pasture and water waiting. Have a safe trip back."

Thomas gave him one of his big self-assured smiles and a nod from his curly blond head hiding under his ten-gallon Stetson.

CHAPTER 12
TRAIN TO UTAH TERRITORY

The newlyweds were boarding the Union Pacific, heading back to Salt Lake in their private car. Flowers and a big basket of fresh fruit from Mr. Ralston were waiting for them in their car.

"Mr. Ralston is a wonderful friend—honest, caring, and successful," Thomas said. "Let's invite him and his family out for a rodeo and a barbecue in their honor."

"Thomas, that is a wonderful idea; they will get to see how we do things out here in the 'wilderness.'" Katryn chuckled. "Perhaps they can return with us after we deliver their cattle in September and stay through the holidays?"

"Yes, Katryn, that will be fun. Let's send them a letter inviting them for the holidays. It starts to snow in the mountains around late September. We can take the narrow-gauge railway up to Casper's Glacier, stay at Father's cabin, and go sleigh riding and cross-country skiing with those big clumsy checkered cross skis."

"Oh, what a blast we will all have, darling. " I will pen a letter to Mrs. Ralston and John Gaynor tomorrow," Katryn said.

"Katryn, do I need to know about your and John's relationship? Do you still love him?"

"No, and no more. Just you, my darling hunk," Katryn responded with a wink.

There was a brisk knock at their door, and Von, the porter in a navy-blue uniform and hat, entered with egg salad sandwiches, German potato salad, and a tall pitcher of lemonade.

"I ordered lunch for us, darling, in our car, so we could spend some quality time and perhaps retire for a nap. There is going to be a big soiree this evening for supper honoring our return. My industrious card buddies arranged it," Thomas announced.

"I do not know whether to be happy or sad, chéri. Those boys are pranksters and nearly drove me dizzy with their antics last time," Katryn uttered.

"Please attend, my beautiful, awesome wife. I simply will be lost without you. And their wives will be very disappointed. They love your New York stories."

"Thomas," Katryn said in a firm voice, "promise me we will leave by midnight. I have something mysterious I want to show you."

"Mysterious! Well, I can't miss such a happening," Thomas exclaimed. "We'll be there for sure. I promise, honey."

As Katryn took a bath and Thomas remained sleeping, she decided to read a magazine from New York while she soaked in warm bubbly luxury.

Once upon a time, there was a castle where a beautiful princess lived. Her name was Marie Antoinette Hapsburg, with hair spun of white gold, cheeks flushed with cherries, lips dipped in wine, magnificent almond-shaped eyes the color of blue sapphires, and a smile that melted men's hearts. What more could a mother ask for!

Little Marie's parents were the emperor and empress of Austria and ruled the Holy Roman Empire in the name of the House of Habsburg, which ruled for over 640 years. This honor was bestowed upon them by the pope, or a vote by other princes called the electors or both. So when the king of France, Louis XV, went looking for a royal wife for his son the dauphine, he chose the most influential royal house in Europe, the Habsburgs. The daughters were easy on the eyes: all blonde, buff, and beautiful, and connected to the Vatican. Their mothers and fathers were Holy Roman emperors.

In her early teen years, Marie spent her time riding horses, learning all the latest dances, attending weddings and funerals, participating in fundraisers for war widows and orphans, planning the St. Mary's Church bazaar, and playing with her pug, Mops—a very busy young woman indeed!

Playing with Mops was her favorite pastime. She would dress her up like a princess, take her for long walks around the palace holding on to her diamond-studded leather leash and collar, sing her songs, read her stories from her diary, and take her for rides in the royal carriage.

When it came time for Marie to marry the dauphine of France— King Louis XV's son and heir to his throne, she realized that little Mops could not join her—ever! It was customary for a new queen in a foreign land to adopt all the new country's customs. Thus, Mops would be replaced with a French poodle. But Marie refused to leave her beloved Mops behind. She commissioned her foreign secretary, Franz Dumont, to smuggle Mops into his carriage and then secretly carry her across the Austrian, Swiss, and French borders, and then take her through a hidden passage that led to the princess's apartment on the south side of the second floor of the Palace of Versailles, outside of Paris.

Soon, Mops became the belle of the palace! She accompanied her mistress everywhere: to parties, balls, dinners, picnics, the theater, Mass, and Paris shopping sprees for chapeaus, ball gowns, lingerie, and sparking diamonds. Little Mops had her own diamond tiara—a little extravagant when the French people were starving for crumbs. About the only activity, Mops did not partake in was receiving Holy Communion. She tasted everything else the princess ate.

Mops woke Her Majesty in the morning by licking her cheeks until she opened her blue eyes. And it was Mops who watched her bathe and get ready for the balls. Furthermore, it was Mops who sat on her bed every night listening to what she wrote in her diary, and it was Mops who sat by her mistress during her final hours while she awaited the guillotine. Mops was spared, thank God. Even though she wanted to join Marie in the afterlife, she did mysteriously disappear forever.

"Thomas, darling! Wasn't that a cute magazine story about our little Mops' namesake who lived at Versailles with Marie Antoinette before the French Revolution?"

"Yes, Katryn," Thomas answered once he had awakened from his nap. "We are very fortunate to have our very own royal princess of a pug."

"I wonder if all pugs have the same inclinations and habits?" asked Katryn.

"Well, I guess we will just have to wait and see," he replied.

"But Mops disappeared and never was found," Katryn exclaimed. "Do you suppose, Thomas, she went into another world and tiptoed into our hearts? Several books have been written about a character falling asleep, waking up, and finding themselves in the future with their home in ruins and their family dead."

"Just fiction, my dear wife," Thomas replied. "Mops is Mops, born in this century. Just check her pedigree."

"Darling, Mops doesn't have one. The owner's note said she just showed up on his doorstep."

Katryn's baby blues sparkled with suspense and intrigue, and peered right into Thomas's smiling eyes.

"So, you think we have a hundred-plus-year-old dog? Not possible." He chuckled at his wife's imagination; he could tell by her eyes what she was thinking. And she was serious!

Katryn was not amused. She excused herself before losing her temper and retired to the mistress's bathroom suite to bathe and dress with the help of her maid. Thomas's gambling friends were not kind when they drank—and they drank morning till night. She wanted to look perfect for their dinner reception, toasting their marriage once again—any excuse to party and drink. These city folks hadn't a clue as to what good old-fashioned hard work was like, how complete one felt after putting in a hard day's work like she and Thomas did daily to give their family a comfortable and healthy lifestyle.

There were no corner grocery stores, she thought, to buy milk and bread out in the wilderness of Utah Territory. Milk came from first milking the cow's teats, then separating the heavy cream with a wooden paddle before bringing it in from the barn and cooling it off with blocks of ice that were chopped from the pond's winter freezes and then saved in sawdust down in the cold cellar until desired. The bread came from kneading yeast, flour, lard, sugar, salt, eggs, and baking powder together in a deep round bowl; setting the dough aside twice; punching it down with one's fist twice; allowing it to rise; and then baking it in the oven. It was not an easy process, especially the butter, which took hours to churn, but in the end, it was all worth it when one bit into a thick slice of soft, warm bread with a shiny egg-wash crust, freshly made with sweet butter spread on top and washed down the esophagus with a glass of cold milk. *Yum! There is an unparalleled satisfaction in having made something yourself—a sweetness all its own.* Katryn chuckled to herself. *I love Mormon living. It is so original and organic.*

The party was bittersweet but ended on a happy note, with the gang promising to throw the Huntzmons another party once a year, same place, same time. On the next occasion, all their children were invited to attend, and they would all go bird-watching at Golden Gate Park, sail on Jonathan's yacht, and tour San Francisco Bay, plus go swimming in the Pacific Ocean. *Sounds like a plan!* Katryn and Thomas thought.

The Union Pacific pulled into the station at Salt Lake, and the entire Huntzmon clan was there to greet them.

"Did you have a good time, Son?" Martin asked with a wink.

Thomas smiled and winked back. "Father, you're going to be a grandfather. I'm sure of it."

"Yippee!" Martin yelled as he took off his hat and flung it up in the air. "And his name will be Thomas Martin V. Just like my great-grandfather."

Thomas's mother gave him and Katryn each a warm hug and asked if they were hungry.

"I brought some fresh apricot scones and buttermilk for the trip back," Esther said.

As they all drove back to the ranch, the newlyweds described their honeymoon with many giggles and exaggerated descriptions of the Palace Hotel and all its grandeur, especially the furnishings. They also elaborated on the clothing and floral emporiums and the French and Chinese restaurants they visited in San Francisco. No mention of an old beau of Katryn's. *Very interesting,* Thomas thought.

The Huntzmon ranch could be seen on the horizon at last. It had been a long five-hour drive with a lunch stop by Mountain Meadows. It was there that Martin had told of the senseless massacre of innocent men, women, and children over eight years old that had occurred on September 11, 1857.

"The church has been repenting ever since," he said. "It was a big mistake and a misunderstanding, and I don't want to discuss it. The church has moved on, and so have I."

"The Huntzmon ranch at last!" Katryn said.

Everyone from Thomas's ranch and his parents gathered around and cheered the couple on as they drove up to the main house. Thomas picked up his new bride and carried her over the threshold—a Mormon tradition. The Relief Society sisters were in the house. They greeted the newly married couple. Katryn wanted to help, but they would not permit it. "Just go upstairs to your bedroom. We fixed it up very Victorian style with lots of white lace ribbons, a white-fringed knotted wedding quilt, and lots of white desert lilies." Thus Katryn's Mormon life began as a wife and mother and later as the St. George's Women's Relief Society president. She was not an innocent girl when she met and married the one. Except for her virtuous condition, Miss New York City was very street-smart, and she knew men, politics, and religion and how to get what she wanted, especially when it came to the male species. But the Western Mormon man was a real piece of work for her to figure out; he was righteous and generous to a fault and independent as hell, albeit needy when it came to women. The Western Mormon man was patient with children's shortcomings, very supportive of his family's dreams and endeavors, and intriguingly mysterious. There were lots of times when Thomas would disappear for days, only to return from the church duty he had performed upon receiving the call of Brigham Young. "Men, do your duty" was a favorite Mormon axiom to inspire the priesthood to perform religious tasks with vim and vigor and with a positive spiritual attitude. Katryn knew that Thomas Huntzmon was not an easy target to mold into the gentleman her father was: a well-dressed man of high moral fiber and breeding. She loved Thomas just the way he was, loving, gentle, tough, and righteous. In the bedroom, he was a pussycat and lion rolled into one muscled hunk of flesh.

On the other hand, Thomas was not intimidated by his wife's intelligence; instead, he embraced her medical knowledge. She'd mended many a broken arm and leg around the ranch, started a young women's group in the church to minister to the sick and penurious, raised money and supplies for widows and single mothers, taught first aid and midwifery classes and found the time to birth nine children, one of whom died on the way to the Arizona Mission—but that would come later.

CHAPTER 13
THE MORMON WAY

Life as a Mormon wife was bittersweet for Katryn. It seemed she conquered baking, quilting, and having babies, but practicing the Word of Wisdom—part of the Mormon dogma—was challenging for her. It made no sense to forbid hot drinks when it was freezing cold outside. She would just die if she couldn't enjoy drinking exotic coffees as she had done in New York, Paris, and Italy. *Simply outrageous,* Katryn thought. She also hated wearing the cumbersome one-piece garment in the hot summers. Sometimes she would sneak off and swim, watching it hang from a sagebrush bush as she used its red ribbons to tie up her blonde curls on top of her head. *Oh well, no one is perfect at first. Doing something new and getting to like it takes time,* Katryn kept reminding herself. But she was determined to improve herself and follow the Word of Wisdom.

"Thomas, the Mormon ways are too strict for me, but I made a covenant with God that I shall keep if it kills me."

"It won't kill you, darling. Just persevere, and your rewards will be many beautiful, healthy children and a continual smile on my face," he said while chuckling.

Thomas was patient and always encouraged Katryn to be perfect. He used to say to her, "You can do it, sweetheart. Keep trying." Then she would try more arduously than before. But Katryn knew in her heart that she would never be a perfect Mormon, at least not in this lifetime. Her previous life was fun, lavish, adventurous, and never boring, whereas her present life could be all that too, except when children entered the picture. Sacrifices became the norm. Dreams of traveling eastward were put on a back burner. There was no time for a mani and pedi; nails were filed by herself. Her hair was combed with vinegar or rinsed with lemon juice and brushed up in a bun, covered with a pioneer bonnet, instead of her having a perfumed shampoo and the latest Parisian updo.

Life started to get complicated once the children came. Katryn's time wasn't her own; she was too tired to play amorously with her husband when he was home. The children took so much care and discipline. She just didn't know how to delegate the domestic chores to the servants. But in time, she would learn.

Over the next ten years, Katryn spent her days in her huge salmon-colored tiled kitchen, mostly wearing a white ruffled apron over a modest blue cotton dress with deerskin boots adorning her tiny angelic feet. There was a sewing room where, on occasion, Katryn darned everyone's socks and mended their rips and made her daughters' dresses and her sons' shirts. Jeans for everyone came from a Montgomery Ward catalog that was delivered by rail and then brought out to the ranch by the postman on horseback or a buckboard drawn by two horses.

Furthermore, Katryn's life was very scheduled after the kids came. Monday evening was when the family stayed home together. Katryn spent all day kneading yeast rolls, slowly boiling venison stew, and baking apple cherry cobbler for her family. Once supper was over—about 6:00 p.m.—the entire family of nine gathered in the barn. Sitting on hay bales on both sides of the loft with kerosene lamps hanging from hooks and musical instruments in each child's hand, the Huntzmon clan would begin to make beautiful music. Casey, Thomas's Australian cow dog, would howl along. It sounded off-key, but no one cared. They were having too much fun.

Tuesday was washday. Thomas always started a fire in the backyard and then placed a big copper kettle on top. Also, he had made a long wooden paddle to flip-flop the clothes. Katryn would pour bleach and shaved lye soap into the pot, pick up the paddle, beat the clothes, rinse and wring them, and then hang them on twelve clotheslines with help. "Big families call for drastic measures," Thomas would always say when the older children would complain about hanging too many clothes.

Wednesday was grandparents' day. Everyone went to the Bozemon ranch to visit Grandma Esther and Grandpa Martin. They were getting up in age, so everyone pitched into clean the house, bailing hay, feed animals, brush horses, trimming the horses' hooves, ironing shirts, and cooking a pot of beans with fatback. Katryn would bring some of her delicious beef stew, apple cherry cobbler, and yeast rolls from Monday's supper to share.

Thursday was ironing and darning socks day. The supper was homemade noodles and beef chunks with gravy. Thomas would read the Book of Mormon after dinner. Katryn would read Bible stories to her four youngest children, who were all under six years.

Friday was the young men's meeting at St. George Temple on the north side. Occasionally, on Fridays, Thomas and his father would drive to Salt Lake to meet secretly with Brigham Young and then return to their home in the morning. Katryn would stay home and bake bread and fruit tarts for her family and in-laws. She only made pies and cakes for birthdays and holidays.

Saturdays were spent at home cleaning the house and caring for the animals.

Saturday evening was bath night and time to prepare for church. Everyone took turns bathing the twins and laying out their church clothes.

Sunday was Lord's Day—no work! The family attended Sacrament Meetings and Sunday school, as well as the Relief Society for women and the Melchizedek and Aaronic priesthoods for men. Once the Huntzmons returned home, they would rest and enjoy Sunday supper together. Bedtime came early for this hardworking family—8:00 p.m. sharp.

Sunday evenings were for Thomas and Katryn to enjoy some quality time together. No one was permitted to disrupt their tranquility. The happy couple would take a bubble bath together in the winter. In the summer, they would sneak up to the cool pond and make mad passionate love behind the trickling waterfall.

As time passed, Katryn was getting used to following Mormon dogma. She no longer swam in rivers without church garments; she kept the Word of Wisdom and raised her children to love the Lord, the Mormon Church, family, and others; and she planned to send all her children on a mission before marriage and college.

From the children, Thomas was hoping for a self-righteous cowboy—typical rancher—while Katryn was hoping one of their gems would become a doctor or lawyer (typical Jewish mother). Although someone would have to inherit the Huntzmon ranch and run it with an iron fist, neither Katryn nor Thomas were worried. The ranch practically ran itself. There were birthing cribs in the barn, corrals for branding and cutting, and three sections (640 acres each) of green pastures and three mountain streams for natural nourishment. The sale of crossbred cattle (Herefords and Texas longhorns) brought in over two million dollars' profit yearly and one million dollars from the sale of fine wool from Katryn's thousand rambouillet ewes crossed with white-faced merino sheep—a highly coveted combination that produced fine silky wool.

Ranching came with responsibilities: feed others, kept cattle alive, irrigation, conserve water, and replenish the earth. Any one of Katryn and Thomas's offspring could run the ranch. The children did house chores from age three, working long hours alongside their siblings and picking up rocks from the fields. Then they milked cows, sheared sheep, branded cattle, planted alfalfa, and nurtured a vegetable garden with irrigation ditches by the age of eleven. So, when the time came for someone to step up and run the ranch, there would be plenty of Huntzmons with the right skills to choose from.

One summer day, Thomas went home early for lunch. He flung open the kitchen door and saw Katryn bending over the wash sink. He started to walk toward her and then quickly stopped. She turned around and smiled.

"Don't you come near me with that passionate grin; I'm warning you."

"But, darling, little Thomas needs to see his little baby doll."

"Not now, my macho man, who is always ready to make love, is never tired, exudes an overabundance of energy, does fifty push-ups in five minutes, wrangles two horses simultaneously, and adds meaning to my world. But today is washday, honey: twenty pair of pants, twelve undergarments, ten shirts, and fifteen pairs of socks. And they all must be ironed," Katryn managed to say in one breath.

"Even the socks?" Thomas asked with a chuckle.

"No, silly, but everything else does. And then, after all that, I will make my first-place Washington County Fair chili con carne with my mouthwatering jalapeño cornbread. And somewhere between cooking and eating supper, I must do some important planning for Sunday's Relief Society meeting."

"Well, Katryn, you are my Renaissance gal. How may I help?" Thomas asked.

"Would you please collect ten hymnals and two church trivia games while I finish preparing supper? The missionary boys Vaughn and Steve are joining us. That would be an immense help! But for now, my macho man, make me happy by vanishing for two hours."

"Fleur-de-lis, my sweet!" he responded.

And off he went, riding his horse into the purple sunset to feed the cattle some corn. He didn't go too far since they were about a five-minute ride away, tucked in a canyon so no rustlers could steal them. Cattle rustling was prominent when water was scarce, causing cattle to die or to be slaughtered early.

Six o'clock came soon enough. The missionaries were early and helped the boys feed the chickens, pigs, and goats. The girls set the table with a white Irish linen and lace tablecloth with matching napkins, Grandma's fine pink rosebud Austrian China, Aunt Donella's crystal goblets, and a floral centerpiece from Thomas's garden of blue-ribbon long-stem crimson roses. Katryn was very particular about how her table looked—her goal was to exude grace, elegance, and beauty.

"God help you if you spill anything on it or break a dish!" she would yell, which no one did.

At six o'clock sharp, Thomas led prayers of thanksgiving. He passed out cornbread while Katryn scooped out the chili con carne in Southwestern coral and turquoise ceramic bowls. Throughout the mouthwatering meal, all the children took turns discussing their day. Sarah and Drucilla had had a fight over a stuffed bear; Morgan and Calvin squirted goat milk at each other; and Lizette visited Grandma Esther and helped tie her new quilt. The older two boys, Thomas Jr. and Galvin Lee, helped their dad look for some stray cows, which they wrangled back to the barn. And the two missionaries spoke of their day helping the grandparents plant potatoes, carrots, and squash. Steve remarked how delicious Lizette's cherry pie was with sweet cream on top. And Vaughn, who was twenty pounds overweight, just yawned.

"Hey, Vaughn, wake up, or I will eat your pie," Steve said.
"Not on your life, Cousin," he replied.

"Now, now, boys, there is plenty of pie; I made three of them since I know cherry is your favorite, especially you, Vonny. May I call you Vonny?" Lizette added with a wink. Vonny's cheeks turned bright red. A romance started to bloom from a piece of Lizette's pie. And with a sprinkle of grace from above, a great love developed that spawned many generations of Nelsons.

CHAPTER 14
THE TWENTIETH ANNIVERSARY OF THE MOUNTAIN MEADOWS MASSACRE

Katryn Kline Wellington Huntzmon, lying in a St. Mark's hospital bed after giving birth to twins for the second time, found a recent newspaper to read that made her pass out—something she hadn't done while giving birth to her twins.

The *Salt Lake Tribune*'s headliner for September 11, 1877, read: "Twentieth Anniversary of Mountain Meadows Massacre—FACT or FICTION?" The victims' names were listed according to three categories: men, women, and children, and there was also a list of survivors under eight years old.

After Mountain Meadows Massacre—three days to be exact—there was a second wagon train that was guided by Mormons in the night so the party couldn't see the naked dead bodies strewn all over the cold, hard ground. Even though they had heard about the Indian Massacre, they didn't know the entire truth—that Mormons and Natives from southern Utah Territory had helped kill 120 men, women, and children over six. The trail of blood led to the prophet Brigham Young—despite a letter he wrote after the fact that advised that the Natives be left to do what they wanted to do with the emigrants but that Mormons, on the other hand, were not to harm these Gentiles. Instead, Brigham instructed them to help them on their way to California by providing food, but nothing meant for their livestock since grain was scarce that year.

This group was the wealthy Fancher party from Arizona before it had to be divided because of wagon repairs and having too many cows to graze at one time. One hundred twenty emigrants headed southwest toward the California Trail. They camped forty miles west of Cedar City in a meadow four miles by two miles in size; there were two streams, plenty of pasture, a couple of ravines, and many hills and trees—an ideal resting place for pioneers on their way to California.

Located one and a half miles southwest of the meadows was a Mormon leader and Indian agent, Jacob Hamblin, whose calling was to smooth relations between American Indians and Mormon settlers.

Jacob Hamblin's ranch house and huge corral were where these pioneers, part of the Fancher party from Arkansas, camped in a circle, filling in all the wheels with dirt and digging trenches to make a fort with mud and sand to protect themselves from the Paiute tribe. Some Mormons, dressed in disguise, changed clothes down by Corn Creek and attacked, shot, and killed a few emigrants who had stood their ground for five to seven days.

The story in the *Salt Lake Tribune* stated that word was sent from a church higher-up that a plan was to be set in motion that would make the emigrants think that the Mormon militia would protect them from harm by walking beside each one—acting as their guard—but there was a hitch: these Arkansans had to turn in their weapons, guns, and knives and innocently follow the Mormon militia to their demise and slaughter. This military group also worked to protect parts of the Western United States—California, Arizona, Utah, New Mexico, and Texas—before 1892. These poor innocent travelers had no clue that they would quickly hear an officer's voice from the militia say, "Men, do your job!" And so, the bloody, gory slaughter began. Almost every emigrant man was killed, but three—two escaped running but were later shot by Natives, and one was caught in Las Vegas. It was said by the Natives there that he was brutally tortured by four Mormons, possibly using blood atonement for the atrocities inflicted on the saints in Missouri and for the killing of Parley Pratt in Arkansas, who was one of Brigham's apostles. So naturally, he got the blame at first, but John D. Lee later confessed. He was the only one shot for planning and carrying out the plot.

"What about the children who lived through the atrocities?" Katryn asked Thomas, who was sitting near her bed.

"They were all found except for one boy who lived among the Navajo Nation, south of the Utah Territory. The rest were returned to their families in Arkansas over time, my darling."

"Oh, Thomas, I am speechless. How could something like this have happened? I thought Mormons were above reproach. Those poor victims trusted the Mormon militia; if we can't count on them, who can we trust? I'm mad as hell; I want answers. Perhaps we should join the Baptists?"

"Now, darling, our church is true, but sometimes the people in it aren't. We just can't drop the truest religion this side of the Atlantic Ocean because of an error in judgment."

Katryn hugged Thomas and sobbed for hours while rocking in his arms. Then she passed out from exhaustion and shock. He knew the massacre was a dark spot in the Mormon religion, one that would haunt them forever. Thomas remembered his grandfather Jacob speaking about it during a priesthood meeting like it was yesterday:

"Brothers, we must instruct our young men not to make the same mistake against emigrants like the Fancher party from Arkansas. We will treat all travelers with respect, assist them when their wagon wheels break and share fresh food and water for their journey westward."

He received a standing ovation. Thomas recalled how proud he was to be his grandson.

Katryn was sleeping now, so Thomas decided to reread the article. He noticed it didn't say anything about the two children Hamblin had taken in. One of the infants had half his arm shot off by accident, and the other, a three-year-old, was intact. *Thank God!* Thomas thought. He put the paper down and went to sleep himself. The next morning at breakfast, nothing was said about the article. Thomas and Katryn had promised each other never to speak of it again.

It had been twenty years since this dark time, and everyone had moved on. Sometimes journalists liked to stir things up to sell more papers or magazines.

God is great, God is good, and God believes in *justice*!

CHAPTER 15
THE WOMEN'S RELIEF SOCIETY

The Mormon Women's Relief Society was started by Emma Smith and supported by her husband and Prophet, Joseph Smith. This society evolved from providing for the temporal and spiritual needs of Mormon widows and orphans and expanded to midwifery, nursing the sick, and finding shelter for the homeless. The trip from the East into an untraveled wilderness in Northern Mexico was not easy. The trip to Zion could be treacherous on occasion with Native American raids. Many men, women, and children died along the trail because of cholera, dysentery, pneumonia, and accidents. Wagons broke down when following many trails that went through forests and over rocks and rivers, causing parties to slow their pace and hit snow even though they had left early enough to beat the winter. Some people stayed behind to wait for the Mormon militia to rescue them, only to die in a blizzard. On one such occasion, the militia arrived too late; they found many people frozen where they had fallen, sat down, or gone to sleep. It was common to see long braids of young teenage girls frozen to the ground or heroic mothers covering their dead babies with their skirts to keep them warm. No matter what tragedy occurred, the need for the Relief Society was there, except when Brigham Young arrived in the Salt Lake Valley on July 24, 1847. A hot meal of boiled beef roast, mashed potatoes, carrots, and gravy with yeast rolls would have warmed his and the men's empty bellies. Unfortunately, these holy men didn't have much left in their sacks to eat until they went hunting for deer and foraging for wild berries.

So, when the bishop of Katryn's ward (made up of five hundred families) asked her to accept the calling as Relief Society president of the Saint George stake (a group of ten wards), she was overwhelmed with emotion and doubt. Tears streamed down her frozen face; she was speechless and in shock. *Imagine that,* she thought. The Lord had chosen her to help his people in their time of need. Although she didn't feel worthy, she trusted him to lead the way.

The first order of business was that Katryn chose her assistants. Some were from the Santa Clara Indian Mission to act as midwives since they were experts in childbirth and making herbal poultices to kill pain and extract poisons from infections and snakebites. She also set up training sessions to teach other women in remote parts of southern Utah Territory the same birthing skills. Next, she had to choose nonjudgmental sisters to visit members of the church. Katryn selected only visiting teachers who were humble and who loved to serve the Lord by helping others in need of his blessings. She chose the Swenson identical twins from St. George to organize the women in twelve wards to visit the sick and needy. These sisters distributed food, clothes, and a weekly spiritual message. On occasion, they found warm, loving homes for the homeless and orphans and made huge meals for weddings and funerals. It wasn't uncommon for a woman, after she gave birth, to find a pot of rabbit stew and a fresh loaf of dark rye bread waiting for her on the stove. Katryn's goal was to make everyone feel loved and accepted; it was her nonjudgmental approach.

Not all Mormons followed the Word of Wisdom. Giving up smoking, hard liquor, and coffee during a blizzard was difficult. But soon, people would drink natural Mormon tea with honey collected from a nearby bush or hot cocoa from Mexico. One of Katryn's mottos was, "There is always one more way to skin a cat; just pray about it to the Lord, and he will show you the way."

Katryn loved being president of the St. George's Woman's Relief Society. She and her team of selfless sisters attended daily to the needy, the sick, and the elderly with vim and vigor and with a sincere effort to change the world and make it a better place to live honestly and righteously.

One day Katryn was at the temple, downstairs in the large-gathering activity room, with the Swenson twins and some others tying a wedding quilt as a gift to be placed upon the wedding bed the night of the wedding. This quilt had a bright white background covered with multicolored cotton patches in the shape of a circle looping around it. An old gray wool army blanket was placed in between the front and back covers to ensure warmth on a cold evening. To finish the quilt, Katryn needed many hands to tie each piece of yarn from the back to the front side to turn the quilt into one fiery hearth for two naked bodies to move about on. This magical quilt would be passed down from generation to generation and symbolize good old-fashioned love and fertility.

"Katryn, who is the lucky couple getting this quilt?" Gretchen asked.

"Must keep that a secret. The Prophet is continuing God's work of plural marriage by taking a new wife. He doesn't want his favorite wife, Amelia, to know until it is over. She had a cow the last time he married. Even though she is Brigham's favorite wife because of her elegance, her style of dress, and her ability to play the piano and sing his favorite song, 'Fair Bingen on the Rhine,' Amelia wants to be the only wife he beds. So, mum's the word, Sister Swenson!"

"I promise, my lips are sealed, sister," Swenson replied as she winked.

During her tenure as Relief Society president, Katryn experienced some controversial events she couldn't report to the president of her stake. Some things were too dangerous to know and invaded the privacy of some women. An example of this occurred one evening when she received a note from the Prophet through her stake president, summoning her to leave immediately for his winter quarters on Bleaker Street in St. George near her home. The note read as follows:

Wife number nineteen's birth of her first child is near and rather tenuous. Please hurry; their lives are at stake! You will receive many blessings; just get here as quickly as possible. Godspeed!

Brigham, your prophet
PS: I will be eternally grateful and generous to your cause of the Relief Society.

Katryn arrived in time to assist with a successful birth.

Throughout the ordeal, the mother-to-be was so delirious she cried out bits of secrets between the Prophet and herself—things that shouldn't be repeated. Katryn felt embarrassed and alarmed by what she had heard; she felt the urgency to pray about the couple's marriage and their newborn son, Thaddeus.

Married life was difficult for a husband with fifty-five wives and fifty-seven children, leading the Church of Latter-day Saints, operating multiple businesses, and protecting the saints from physical danger from Gentiles, the government, and any temptation to apostatize nonbelievers of the Mormon faith. But Brigham was a very hard worker, and was also loyal to the church and overprotective of his children. He was proactive on every issue and didn't let trivialities get him down. He was very upbeat, unlike some leaders, such as Abraham Lincoln, who had a mercurial personality. Although the Prophet was rough around the edges sometimes, he kept the church from going bankrupt; expanded the Mormon gospel to Arizona, Nevada, California, and Northern Mexico; and started Brigham Young University—formerly Brigham Young Academy—in Provo and the University of Utah in Salt Lake City.

Katryn congratulated the new mother and left her calling card. She told Mrs. Young that if she should have any complications or need her services, she should send someone around, and Katryn would come back at any hour.

In a few days, such a request came. Katryn returned to check on the mother and baby; she was pleased to find everyone well and ready for afternoon tea, an activity Brigham insisted on for only his wives so they would have a social life without him. Amelia just demanded too much of his attention. And when she beckoned, he did somersaults to please her. This particular wife always made Brigham feel special, wanted, and worthy of her qualities.

"Sister Young, it is so grand to see you so awake and to find Baby Thaddeus so perky. You both look healthy and sharp. His foot has turned completely around and looks normal. Bravo!"

"And, yes, you were there to fix it, Sister Huntzmon. I will forever be grateful. Would you please join me for afternoon tea?

Hattie baked her famous plum scones and mixed a tasty herbal Mormon tea with honey," Mrs. Young said.

Katryn picked up the baby, kissed his plump rosy cheek, and twirled him around and around. Little Thadd just loved it.

After putting him back in his birthing basket, Katryn went over to Ann and hugged her, but first, she touched her forehead, which was cool as a cucumber.

"You clean up grand, Miss Ann, just grand! And little Thadd is a gift from God—so perfect!"

"I love him, Sister Huntzmon, and so does Brigham. He insists on rocking our precious son before bedtime when he is home and always gives him a special blessing. He said our son will become a patriarch of the Church of Latter-day Saints one day after Brigham passes on to eternity."

Katryn was fidgety. She dropped her white linen napkin and cleared her throat.

"Well, Sister Young, during your labor, you yelled out some strange comments."

"Sister Huntzmon, what comments?"

Now Katryn had sweat running down her forehead while her heart beat faster. "I am so embarrassed to say what I am about to say, but during labor pains, you talked about divorcing the Prophet. You didn't mean it, did you, Ann?"

"Oh, is that all? Labor pains bring the truth out in a woman. Well, Katryn, I plead guilty. Yes, indeed, I am divorcing him. My marriage has been a fright ever since he married Amelia. She is so bossy and communicates Brigham's wishes about what duties he bestows upon us other wives. She talks down to us like we are her slaves. And what irritates me is how Brigham enables her to be so cruel. He controls our every move and keeps our curiosity for the outside world in a jar. Plus, he has wanted us barefoot and pregnant for years. I can't remember when I got into my wedding gown. My clothes are shabby and dull. As a wife of the Prophet, I thought I was entitled to maids. I heard that some of the more favored wives slept with Brigham without their church garments and that they had much bigger and better-furnished houses than mine, filled with Irish linen tablecloths and napkins, fine English china, and silver tea sets. And they have their maids to clean, cook, wash, iron clothes, and care for their children. Frankly, I don't know what they do in their spare time. It's not fair, Sister Huntzmon. The Prophet loved me since I was little. He used to hold me on his lap and rock me to sleep. Now he doesn't love me at all. He's downright mean. This winter, I had to beg for my furs. And then there is this business about growing our vegetables. Anything we want, such as beets, squash, and potatoes, must be grown in our garden in the backyard. Brigham generously gives us a piece of beef each month, but it is not enough to feed everyone. Also, we must grind our hamburgers, cut steaks, and kill chickens with these little hands. Look at my blister scars. Disgusting! Just disgusting!"

"Now, Sister Ann, to be fair, all of us sisters must plant our own vegetables. I take great pride in my huge pumpkins. They win at the yearly and make many delicious pumpkin pies topped with fresh whipped cream. Sister Ann, you are just depressed from childbirth. That happens to all of us after we give birth for some reason, and it will pass. How about if some of the Relief Society members help you with your spring planting?"

Ann frowned and twitched her nose as she said, "That would be helpful. Thank you, Sister Huntzmon. But I have told you the truth. Tales travel between maids; they gossip down at Brigham's general store, where I overheard them one morning while I was getting tomato seeds. They were discussing a wife or concubine who used to work in a brothel; she gives Brigham pleasure through her mouth, which is so unladylike."

Katryn, remembering her brothel days, understood perfectly. On many occasions, she and her friend Beatrice watched the women perform their specialties. As a result, sex with her husband, Thomas, was satisfying and eventful for him because of her earlier life working as a seamstress at Frenchie's Emporium of Pleasure. Katryn's life now was less pompous and more righteous; she had found the true church and knew it without a doubt.

The position of Relief Society president demanded strict obedience to Mormon dogma, including the Word of Wisdom. Katryn's commitment to obey grew considerably over her tenure. She successfully took food and clothing to the needy, spread spiritual messages from the Lord and the prophets Joseph Smith and Brigham Young, and birthing babies—even saving the lives of mothers and newborns. The most common cause of death among babies was poor nutrition. The mothers usually died from physical complications like a breech birth, falling off a horse, or falling down the stairs—common techniques practiced among the rich in Europe to prevent having more children. No one would be the wiser! But not here in Utah Territory, where everyone valued children. The more, the merrier!

As Katryn returned home to the ranch, she contemplated what Sister Young had shared and couldn't help wondering if some of the remarks were true. She pondered if the Relief Society could help alleviate postpartum depression. Within a week, Katryn had organized a committee of ten sisters to help new mothers with postpartum depression right in their own homes. These women cooked, washed dishes, organizedmeals, did laundry, etc. Whatever was needed was done by hardworking, compassionate Mormon members of the Relief Society.

CHAPTER 16
KATRYN'S MELTDOWN

Dear Mother and Father,

This Christmas was so depressing; it snowed for two weeks without letting up. These pioneers are used to being snowed in, but this is my first experience. I like looking at all of it, but on the other hand, I would love to take a cruise to Bermuda as we used to every Christmas when I was young. Running in the sand and diving into the refreshing aqua-blue water was fun. Remember when we all would race down to Clément's beach house on our rented bicycles to eat fudge and drink lemonade? Or when we lavished our bodies with coconut lotion after we had lain in the sun for hours and tanned to a dark, wet desert shade? I loved those days. But I know I have a husband and family and must live here in his world now. But forty feet of snow is just too much. We must keep a shovel inside just to get outside to milk the cows and goats and feed the chickens, horses, and pigs. So, when you have lemons, as Grandmother always said, make lemonade, which is my mantra. I have compromised myself so much that I can't even remember when I last took a bubble bath with scented candles.

    Would you believe that—or so Thomas assures me—this is the best time of the year? We are all going to go sleigh riding as soon as the snowdrifts shrink a few feet and visit his parents. They bake so many holiday cookies and fruit cakes Thomas would never miss them. I have baked our famous challah bread to share, that is if there is any left, since your grandchildren have gobbled most of it up during today's breakfast. Good thing I made three loaves, just like Grandma used to do. I prepared the bread just like she did—rich and sweet inside (oil, eggs, and a tad of sugar) with six huge ropes of dough woven together in a thick braid with raw egg brushed on top for a shiny mirrored finish. Very impressive! Everyone loves it sliced with butter and apricot jam. Simply delicious! And yes, we have apricot trees out here in Utah Territory. When we run out of apricots, we have a huge supply from our Romney cousins in Northern Mexico. They have many orchards—papaya, mango, cherry, apricot, apple, pear, orange, grapefruit, and lime. Also, there are many avocado bushes, and the avocados make a wonderful dip with corn tortilla chips. And there is another dip called salsa made of fresh ripened tomatoes, cilantro, white onions, and jalapeños. Simply hot! You can use a little sugar to cut the heat. I will enclose these two recipes. I doubt you can find either of the green veggies, so I will enclose them with some dried cilantro.

I wish you two could share the Christmas holiday with us just once. I hear the train runs daily. Snow just slows it down, but it does run. Just think, in three to four days, you two could be sitting here in my kitchen enjoying a cowboy breakfast on fine blue china. Being boarded up for weeks will change your life forever. You discover things about yourself you never imagined, and you instantly become a game player or go crazy from boredom. We would have tons of fun playing Bible charades where your team tries guessing your favorite Bible verse, checkers, chess, and bingo. There are many books and puzzles for the independent spirit. Come on out and try something different; I promise you will love the Wild West!

I know you are asking yourselves what your darling daughter has learned about herself throughout these trials and tribulations. Honestly, I am very logical and resourceful, which helps me keep my family busy for two weeks while they are blanketed by snow. After the snow stopped, we built a huge snowman, engaged in snowball fights, shoveled paths to our pond so we could ice-skate, and went for many sleigh rides. In the evenings, Thomas built a huge bonfire, and we roasted chestnuts and drank hot cocoa. At midnight, Thomas and I would sneak off for a sleigh ride after the children went to sleep. Our heavens are filled with a gazillion stars out here in Utah Territory; their brightness shines the way for our draft horses to see clearly all the way to the pond.

Well, I must get some sleep. Five o'clock comes early. See you when I see you. And that may be sooner than you think.

Your loving daughter,
Princess

Six o'clock came and went. Katryn just served a hearty breakfast for the snowmen of the house, Thomas, and his newest foreman, Chuck. His previous foreman, Cleaver, had gotten married and was now running his father-in-law's ranch.

"Now, darling, I swear we will have our road cleared and the sleigh ready to go to Mom and Dad's in a couple of hours. Better pack up our gear and bring some snacks like your ginger and sugar cookies. Thanks for that delicious French toast you just made us with lots of butter and syrup. Honey, you're the best baker in St. George. I'm glad I married you."

"Thank you. I love a man who can appreciate something about me other than my good looks and charm. You're a keeper, Thomas Huntzmon. Now go get rid of that snow, pronto!"

The ride to Grandpa's was serene and magical. All the pine trees were covered with white snow, which made their branches resemble angel wings; the barns and the ranch houses had curly white smoke coming out of their chimneys; deer and elk graced the pastures to the woods; and the sky had so many bright diamonds, you could hear them play "Twinkle, Twinkle, Little Star."

The children brought along their guitars and violins and played "Silent Night," "Come All Ye Faithful," and "We Wish You a Merry Christmas." Everyone was jovial and singing these carols, anticipating seeing Opa and Oma. Little Mops sang too. She looked adorable, lying in a red Christmas basket filled with presents for everyone. Katryn had made her a dark green velvet gown and matching hat with a white eagle feather attached on the side. Mops knew she looked pretty, sitting there like the princess she was. Sometimes Katryn could swear the dog was visiting them from another dimension.

"Katryn, mistress of the Huntzmon ranch, we have arrived at our destination; allow me to help you step out of your royal carriage."

"Why, thank you, Mr. Huntzmon, Master of the Purple Plains."

The red door opened, and Opa and Oma greeted everyone.

"Greetings to all! Please come on in, where it's warm. We have spiced hot apple cider with a cinnamon stick and a special guest you all know and love."

As the children looked at each other and rolled their eyes, Thomas grabbed the basket with the presents after he put Mops on her sparkly red leash. Katryn gathered the children and then went inside.

"Mother, is Santa going to find us here at Oma's to give us our presents?" little Tyler asked.

"Yes, children, he will find you here. Please hurry inside where it is warm," Katryn said.

The children ran quickly into the house to see the surprise. There in the middle of the room, next to the fresh blue spruce tree decorated with popcorn, delicate little candled lights, and colorful glass balls hanging from each branch, stood a short, stocky, white-bearded, jolly-looking man wearing a bright red suit and a red hat with white fur trim and a pom-pom on top.

"Santa!" the children yelled as they all went over and hugged him.

It was none other than Thomas's foreman Chuck, who had run around to the back of the house and dressed in Opa's old Santa suit. He was the perfect one to play Ole Saint Nick; he knew all the children by name and knew what they wanted for Christmas. In fact, he had helped Thomas go shopping in Salt Lake and wrapped several toys. Plus, he weighed in at three hundred pounds.

"Let the games begin!" someone yelled.

All the adults sat around the room watching each child go up and sit on Santa's knee and tell him what they wanted for Christmas.

"Merry Christmas, everyone, and especially to all the young'uns," Santa said. "I know you love your presents. Mrs. Claus and I read all your letters and tried to pick out the one present you wanted the most. Thank you for all your delicious food and cookies, Oma. Everything was delicious, as always. We have something very special for you, Oma; it is Mrs. Claus's famous fruitcake with a punch. You will love it," Santa said with a big grin.

"We love you too, Santa and Mrs. Claus. I packed some triple chocolate oatmeal cookies for your trip; I remember how much you both love them."

"Thank you again, Oma, and Godspeed! Must go; lots of children are waiting for me," Santa said.

Opa led everyone in a prayer of thanksgiving and blessed the delicious supper of pork roast, mashed potatoes, and gravy with loads of sauerkraut and applesauce. Katryn served her challah bread with cinnamon butter. A dessert of fresh raspberries over pound cake was a complementary choice. Everyone was licking their fingers for more. In the morning, Oma made delicious French toast from the leftover challah bread. After breakfast, the children went for sleigh rides while the women helped Oma with the dishes, and the men sat around in the living room and told hunting and fishing stories.

Thomas and his father spent some private time discussing something important; Brigham had sent Martin a message saying he was going to be in St. George on New Year's Day and wanted to speak with them. The letter read as follows:

Dear Martin and Your Son, Thomas,

It is of the utmost importance that we meet on New Year's Day for lunch to discuss a matter of life or death. Discretion is a must regarding this meeting!

Respectfully,
Your Prophet, Brigham Young

"Father, what does this letter mean? What does the Prophet want us to accomplish?"

"I think he needs us to persuade the other men to adhere to God's wishes and promote the principle of plural marriage by taking more wives and begetting more children. He wants us to persuade others that polygamy is holy and is the only way to celestial heaven. But let's enjoy ourselves until New Year's. More punch, Son?"

The trip to Oma and Opa's was restful, and most everyone fell asleep after that humongous breakfast. Once back home, Katryn let the children rest while making grilled cheese sandwiches and creamy potato soup. After lunch, chores had to be resumed; it was an ironing day on Thursday. Katryn made sure everyone's Sunday clothes were cleaned, pressed, and hung accordingly. "God is great; God is good; God loves clean and ironed clothes in church," she sang.

There were many wifely chores to do since the children were home from school another week, but Katryn and Thomas loved having them about. And the feeling was mutual. One day soon, each darling would be going off to do their mission and would miss the ranch and Mom and Dad till it ached in the pit of their stomachs. Because of this, spending quality time with each other was very important to the Huntzmons.

Katryn didn't realize it, but her nerves were shot. She was doing too much work and had many domestic and church responsibilities she couldn't complete. She began worrying about Thomas's long nights with his father doing Brigham Young's work, and she thought a lot about Ann Young and her predicament. The stress was too much for her body and mind. Thank God, her mother sent her tickets to meet in New York City and then travel on to their home in the Hamptons next week. Katryn was headed for a complete meltdown.

CHAPTER 17
A TRIP BACK TO NEW YORK

The trip back to New York City was spectacular, with sunny days and cool, breezy evenings. Katryn ate her meals in her room the first few days to meditate on her thoughts. She enjoyed looking at the birds and wild animals and played a little game of counting the prairie dogs that peeped out of their holes in the ground. She forced herself to drink juices and eat raw vegetables and fresh fruit daily. On the third day, Katryn ventured into the dining car for a steak, fried potatoes, and a garden salad. Afterward, she ventured into the Union Pacific Master Library to read the papers. To her surprise, she knew the person of interest on the front page of the *New York Times*. The headline in large Coney Island font read: "Wife number nineteen leaves the Mormon prophet Brigham Young for neglect and mental anguish." The second headline read: "Ann Young sues Brigham Young for millions!" The third headline read: "No alimony!" The first paragraph of that particular article began, "The Prophet claims there will be no alimony awarded to Ann Young since polygamy is not recognized in the federal courts, where this divorce will occur." The fourth headline read: "Brigham Young and Ann living in sin!"

What a scandalous implication! Oh, my goodness! Ann must be nervous, Katryn thought. *I must telegraph her at once. But where is she? Let me read on. Oh yes, she is staying with friends back east. Her lawyer is handling everything by proxy. What does that mean? Will she never return to Salt Lake? Gee, Ann has the courage and gumption to stand up for her beliefs no matter what. And what of the boy? Is he really Brigham's son? I heard rumors of a possible affair with a young Gentile doctor, but that is just a rumor, I'm sure. Oh, there we go; it says here on page 3 that Ann Young will be speaking about the sinful state of polygamy at the Plaza Hotel alongside Harriet Beecher Stowe on May 15 in New York City. The date is not that far off, just a few weeks away. I will make it my business to attend and ask Ann what's happening.* She smirked to herself.

As Katryn turned to page 4, she saw an article titled "Slavery Exists in Utah Territory under the Mask of Polygamy" by Harriet Beecher Stowe. As she read it, she discovered Stowe's comparison of the two types of woman in bondage: one black and one white; one in chains, one without; both depending upon a man for food, clothing, and purpose; and in some instances both having been raped the first time they experienced sex. There were a lot more similarities, but Katryn couldn't read on. She knew that there was some truth to this analysis. And this fact bothered her because she couldn't do anything about it. Perhaps when she returned home, she could proactively treat some of the Prophet's wives and concubines. There were probably others who were in the same boat and also felt helpless. Perhaps she could organize an underground western railroad with the new Union Pacific Railroad that could smuggle women who wanted to escape polygamy and go to California. *I have got to try,* Katryn thought.

Whatever it takes, I am going to try to help these women obtain their independence and live in peace and tranquility somewhere outside of the Utah Territory. Harriet Beecher Stowe is correct: polygamy is evil. It dehumanizes women, makes them feel like second-class citizens, and deflates their self-worth, especially when one once was the youngest wife, only to be replaced by an even younger one. Men just don't realize how sensitive our feelings are. Husbands can be cold and neglectful when courting and wooing a new wife. They expect us wives to help one another when we get cast aside; we're to grin and bear it. Hogwash!

That's where I can help these women, who feel desolate and suicidal and wish to end their lives. I can teach them midwifery skills to support themselves and their children. Babies are being born today, more than ever. Perhaps I can get some women speakers from the East to come out to the ranch and give a seminar on survival skills and tell stories of women who have gained their freedom and enhanced their self-worth. That wedding cabin will do nicely, giving a feeling of freedom in the mountains of the Rockies, where the streams are crystal clear, and the air is the purest. We can listen to great speakers in the meadow nearby and carry a picnic lunch along. I can't wait to meet Harriet Beecher Stowe. I am feeling better already.

The Union Pacific pulled into Union Station on time—twelve noon. As Katryn stepped down from the train, a bevy of her friends surrounded her and cheered her into a carriage drawn by six horses with their necks extended regally above the crowd.

"Katryn, you look grand. Western life must agree with you; your cheeks even glow. Your lips are ruby red, and your skin is firm with no wrinkles," her vain friend Julia remarked.

"It is the peaceful living with God and the fresh mountain water I drink and fresh fruits and vegetables I plant. I even have my own pistachio bush. And the body mask made from red clay does wonders for your skin. It detoxifies as well as nourishes the skin seven layers deep with minerals," Katryn exclaimed.

"What about meat, Katryn? Do you eat meat?" another friend asked.

"Not much. I prefer fresh mountain trout. Also, our Salt Lake has loads of shrimp, and our friend, Mr. Ralston of the Palace Hotel, sends us oysters, Alaskan halibut, and salmon on the train to Salt Lake. My husband takes the buckboard and goes up to the train station to get our parcels of food. Now Thomas is a big meat eater. He swears by it. Pork is his favorite—wouldn't you know, with me being Jewish and all—but to each his own," Katryn stated. "I have learned to make great barbecue pork ribs and baked beans. Very tasty and sweet."

"Ladies, let's go have lunch at Delmonico's. Mr. Wellington is buying," Katryn's mom said. "I hear they have the best steak around, as well their Yorkshire Pudding, and their stuffed baked potatoes are to die for. Those spuds come all the way out West from Idaho, somewhere near you, dear."

"Yes, Mother, I know. I rode the train and ate a few of those tubers. They come down from Idaho by train to Salt Lake and get transported on the Union Pacific. Life doesn't get any better than that, gals, food transported by rail in three to four days instead of a month rotting in the back of a covered wagon."

"Oh, Katryn, you are so fortunate," said Sandra Marie Krieger, her friend from grade school. "May I visit you sometime? Like when you return home, may I accompany you? I want to experience fresh air and clear mountain waterfalls and catch fish and eat them. I'm a poet and shall write poetry about the West, but I must experience it first. Also, I must bring my cat Annabelle, a great mouser. She couldn't stand me leaving her for weeks."

Katryn thought before she opened her mouth. She thought of all the beautiful landscapes Sandra could paint that would spread the word of just how perfect life was out in the Utah Territory. Perhaps she could draw cartoons for the articles she planned to write and get published in the *Salt Lake Tribune* and beyond.

"I think that's a splendid idea, Sandra. You will love painting the Wild West in the open air with beautiful orange-red buttes, purple sage, snow-covered mountain peaks, and waterfalls.

"Yes, you may accompany me back on the train, Sandra Marie. Perhaps Father will loan me his travel car. What do you say, Mom?"

"Sure, he will if he and I can come along. It is time we meet our grandchildren."

"Then it's a deal," Katryn said as she hugged her mother.

"By the way, Katryn, your friends and I have entered you into a debate with two famous women, one from Salt Lake and the other from Ohio."

"Thanks, Mother. I came back here for a stress-free vacation." She chuckled. "So, what are their names, as if I don't already know? Could they be Ann Young and Harriet Beecher Stowe by any chance?"

"How did you know, my lovely daughter, who always has been as smart as a whip?"

"Well, I personally know Ann, and I just read an article that Miss Stowe penned for the *New York Times* comparing slavery to polygamy. It was a thought-provoking article that gave me the inspiration to start my western underground railroad to help qualifying plural wives find healthy locations to live out their lives. Most of them have nine or more children who grow into parents, strong leaders of the priesthood, and faithful members of the seventy."

"Sounds dangerous to me, Daughter. I am your father, and I will tie your limbs to my birch tree in our backyard if I think it will save your life from those 'blood atoners.' You need a solid plan, and I know just the person who can help you, someone who has a private luxurious railroad car that has a clear pass anywhere he wishes it to go. First, we need to set up safe houses near the California Central Valley near San Francisco, near the Union Pacific in Salt Lake, Council Bluffs, and Chicago, and then in New York. Each house can be reached quickly by rail with an accompanying telegraph service. The porters and maids on the trains will be sympathetic for obvious reasons."

"Father, you are magnificent. You are going to become the Train Hero, slipping quietly through hostile territory to bring solace to those who have been oppressed and who wish to be given a second chance to experience freedom. I love how you think." Katryn snickered.

The ladies and gentlemen reached Delmonico's and proceeded to enter the establishment when, lo and behold, Katryn saw a man with dark curly hair checking out her shoes. As he walked over to her, she recognized him.

"Did you leave your riding boots back on the ranch, Mrs. Huntzmon?" Jonathan Gaynor asked.

The Duke interrupted in a loud, jovial voice. "Jonathan, what a pleasure to see you again," he said as the duchess nodded and smiled. "Where have you been hiding all these years? We heard you were killed in South Africa. You look fantastic for a ghost!"

"I made it back in one piece, Duke. I'm sorry to see your daughter, my fiancée, went west and forgot all about me. Katryn broke my heart, Duke; I cried for days. And I don't mind admitting I can get emotional over a female. But I was lucky to find her in California, where I met her husband, Thomas, a very fine human, always providing for his family and helping a friend in need. But I did find one major flaw. He enables our Katryn to be his equal. However, his business acumen is a ten. He is a cattle baron with five hundred thousand crossbreds, one hundred fifty thousand head of sheep, and one hundred fifty quarter horses, by far the richest man west of Chicago and north of Texas. You can be proud of your daughter, Duke; she chose well. I am excited to tell you that I will be going out there in September and staying with my partner, Mr. Ralston. We are going to purchase some of Thomas's fine tender beef for the Palace Hotel, the most luxurious hotel west of Denver. Say, you and the duchess should join us out there, then follow me back to our hotel. We will put you up in the bridal suite, and it will all be on the house. Think about it; you can have a second honeymoon. Katryn and Thomas are joining us. We are all going sailing around the bay with your grandchildren," Jonathan said.

"I don't have to think about such a wonderfully delicious idea. Count us in! We'd love to join you and stay at that famous hotel with that Pied Piper painting I've heard so much about—and the colorful stained-glass roof. Our daughter really enjoyed her stay at your hotel. That is where my first grandson was conceived," said the Duke of Wellington.

"Father, seriously, isn't anything sacred and private with you?" Katryn chuckled.

The waiter came. After seating everyone, including Gaynor, he returned with some iced teas and cold bubbly waters. Out of respect for Katryn's being a righteous Mormon, no one drank alcohol. However, a dessert called for hot coffee and rum for the men and natural lemon ginger tea for the women.

Everyone ordered Delmonico's grass-fed tender prime rib, twice-baked potatoes, and green peas with toasty garlic bread. The plates at Delmonico's were oval-shaped; each held a sixteen-ounce piece of beef with plenty of room for the fixings. The surroundings were elegant and comfortable, with hanging chandeliers, mahogany-backed chairs, white tablecloths, crystal glasses for wine and water, and an aperitif of peppermint schnapps set on every table.

"Ladies and gentlemen! I would like to make a toast to my beloved wife and sweet daughter. May they live longer than me and enjoy life to the fullest. May their dreams become realities, and may my grandchildren prosper! I will always love you both for all eternity. May God bless you!"

Frenchie and Katryn just cheered as they held up their glasses of white grape juice, then drank, bottoms up.

Jonathan made a toast, praising none other than Katryn for dumping him and giving him the freedom to search for his greatest challenge, designing the greatest US hotel of the century, the Palace Hotel in San Francisco.

"You made me immortal, my friend Katryn, and for that, I will forever be grateful," Jonathan said. "If there is anything you need from me, all you need to do is ask, and your wish will be granted, my sweet."

Duke's eyes went to the back of his head as if to grab an idea. With a sinister smile on his face, Duke spun his web.

"Jonathan," said Duke, "I know something she needs to ask you for. Tell him, honey, about your underground railroad. You need a place in San Francisco to house some ladies wanting to escape polygamy and their abusive husbands."

"Mr. Gaynor, my father is providing my railroad car to transport these bullied women to destinations that are safe from slavery. Do you think the Palace Hotel would be willing to help by housing ten women at a time? I would be very grateful if you could grant this request, Jonathan," Katryn said.

"As I said before, ask and you shall receive. Can we have lunch tomorrow and discuss the details, Katryn?"

"Yes, I would like that. We are staying at the Plaza Hotel. Say noon. And we are in the Royal Suite."

"Perfect!" Jonathan replied.

Dinner ended at 10:00 p.m., and Katryn decided to retire early. Tomorrow was going to be a big day for her, and she wanted to be her best. She had even rescheduled lunch with her former fiancé, John Gaynor, until the next day.

Katryn awoke late in the morning, feeling rested and eager for the day to unfold. Her big debate was tonight, and she needed to prepare and look her best. A vanilla bubble bath was the perfect retreat; she could collect her thoughts on what she would say and cleanse herselfsimultaneously. The debate was to be held in the library of the Astor House at 7:00 p.m.

CHAPTER 18
THE GREAT WOMEN'S DEBATE OF APRIL 1875

Katryn was calm and collected as she sat, patiently waiting for the debate to commence. Her notebook was stuffed with practice questions. A young woman named Deborah with honey-blonde hair, about twenty years old, passed out the debate rules, handing each contestant a white piece of paper.

"Please read the rules and raise your hand if you have any questions," she said. "Good luck, everyone! The debate will start in ten minutes."

The Debate Rules

A question must be answered in three minutes or less.

Points will be given for clarity, elocution, poise, accuracy, appearance, and the degree of the audience's response—five points each, with a total of thirty points.

Fighting, pulling hair, or scratching the eyes is not permitted.

The prize for the winner with the most points is a fuchsia-pink box filled with French designer perfume, powder, and bath salts, plus a huge heart-shaped box of chocolate-covered cherries and a bottle of vintage red wine—to enjoy with a hot bath.

It was 6:45 p.m.; the spacious rectangular room was packed with the elite of New York City society. The audience was focused, the clock was ticking loudly, and the contestants were nervous, with beads of sweat dripping down their foreheads.

The announcer was Bishop Terrance, head of the infamous New York City parish located in the colorful Tenderloin District—filled with streetwalkers, brothels, Irish pubs, and many homeless single mothers and their babies from one-night stands.

As Katryn was sitting patiently, waiting for her question, she reminisced about her early brothel days when she and her friend Pinkie would peek through the curtains and watch the sexy boudoir shows or when she mended Miss Kittie's torn negligees—her johns became overzealous while fondling her breasts. Katryn proudly smiled when she thought how far she had come in society from that rat-infested district in Lower Manhattan. She chuckled to herself. *There is light at the end of the tunnel. I am happily married to my soul mate, Thomas, carrying his third child in my womb, sitting in front of the Sacred Four Hundred, New York's finest and richest, and going to win the debate—not shabby for a Tenderloin girl. It doesn't get any better than this.*

Bishop Terrance banged his gavel, and the long-awaited debate commenced. His eyes focused intently on the contestants.

"We will begin with Ann, then move on to Harriet, and finally hear from Katryn. And then the order will reverse: Harriet, Katryn, and Ann," the bishop announced. "Question number one: Please define polygamy."

Ann answered, "A marriage between one man and more than one wife who will remain married for all eternity."

Harriet said, "An abomination where the wife gives herself to one man, promising to be faithful and obedient, whereas the husband can marry as many wives as he chooses."

Katryn said, "A loving marriage where there is one husband and many sister wives who help each other with domestic chores and share conjugal visits per a schedule made out by the head wife—usually the first wife."

Bishop Terrance replied, "Thank you, ladies. Those were

excellent responses." As he wiped the sweat off his brow, he looked around the room and saw a crowd filled with a hunger for the delicious but decadent tales of the oppressed Mormon women.

"Question number two," he said. "What are the benefits of polygamy?"

Harriet replied, "Bishop Terrance, it would work against all women if I gave one ounce of credence to that question. Just uttering that diabolical word sends me to hell and back. It stands for white slavery of the most cunning and sinister kind. Mormon wives, like black slaves, have no control over their futures. Their astute opinion doesn't count, and they work day and night with hardly a minute's rest, without compensation, and without their husband's appreciation—just like the Southern black slave. There has always been the exceptional slave owner whose compassion and Christian spirit inspired him to treat his slaves with dignity and respect—he taught them to read the Bible, write their name, and do figures—and upon their demise, gave them the most precious of gifts, their freedom."

Katryn answered, "The benefits are that the Lord's divine principle of plural marriage is being exalted, and many souls can be born to proselytize Mormon dogma. Strong and fulfilling comradeship among the sister wives occurs by sharing and by assisting with birthing, baking, cooking, milking, and schooling of the children. I will admit sharing one's husband can be difficult at first, but the positives outweigh the negatives, or so I am told by many polygamous wives. For the record, I am my husband's only wife. I have enjoyed my husband's nights away from conjugal duties when he is on cattle trips—I have plenty of reading and writing letters to catch up on."

Ann answered, "I agree with Sister Katryn, but I would like to add that a huge basket of warm unconditional love and understanding develops among the sisters. Of course, there is always that one wife who can only see life through her dark-colored lenses—selfish, self-centered, and narcissistic to the end, regardless of circumstances!"

Bishop Terrance said, "Thank you, ladies, for your explicit responses. Maybe a bit much on the criticism, but definitely interesting nevertheless."

He said, "Now for question three: What are the negatives of polygamy?" Katryn replied, "Some of the negatives of polygamy, I was told by the women in the Relief Society, is not feeling your husband's warm body next to yours nightly. A cold, lonely gap develops that will never be filled, and that saddens a wife, even though she understands why. Another negative occurs among sister wives when the first wife goes through culture shock when 'I' becomes 'we.' A second wife shows up, and her husband is no longer just hers. She now must share conjugal visits. Different foods appear on the table, and wife number one starts to have more free time in the evening. The worst experience of adding a new wife is that every decision must be shared among the wives. But the hardest feeling to control for plural wives is jealousy, which develops when they see their husband courting a new prospective wife. He showers her with kisses and presents and makes the sister wives wait on her every whim so she may feel welcome and unintimidated by their presence. The new wives are usually much younger girls—fourteen and sexually inexperienced—and vulnerable to criticism by their elders. And dealing with a wife much younger than you is painful but manageable, especially knowing that one day she will be the jealous one. But you only accept that after crying yourself to sleep on many cold and lonely nights."

Ann said, "Well, my worst experience was getting no sex when it was my night. I was anticipating it and had prepared my body with expensive creams and French perfume, but it was all for nothing. My husband didn't show, and I received no explanation as to why. And it is not proper to ask. So, I was very saddened and worried because it is important to me that I provide our heavenly Father with many warriors to spread his principle and Holy Scriptures. Hence, I can't accomplish my spiritual responsibilities when I skip a beat. I didn't have as many children as God wanted because of my husband's neglect. And I hate him for this."

Harriet said, "So poignant and predictable, Ann. The thing I see happening after hearing what you described, is that a woman's right to life, liberty, and pursuit of happiness is being violated, especially if the husbands take on very young wives around the age of fourteen. I'm sorry, but that is child abuse. It is unconscionable and shouldn't be allowed if you love yourself, which is obviously a moot point since you Mormon sisters have low self-esteem and haven't a clue what the world is doing around you, including Gentile women, whom you are not permitted to converse with because they follow the Bible and not the Book of Mormon. Tell me something, Ann and Katryn, can your husbands marry two women at the same time, for instance, twins? Does he get to sleep with both simultaneously?"

A roar of laughter and clapping rose in the audience.

"Hey, this is turning into a delicious catfight. Have at it, ladies," someone in a red plaid shirt yelled from the last row.

Bishop Terrance raised his voice, "Ladies, control yourselves. Let's start with question four: Do you see a similarity between slavery and polygamy? If so, give examples."

Ann replied, "I see no difference except the color of our skin. I was made to work as a field hand with many pussy blisters to put vegetables on my table for my children. I also had to make their clothes and beg for furs to cover all our frail bodies on those cold and snowy winter days. Brigham rarely saw his adopted children from my first husband or me as his harem grew."

Harriet said, "Believe me, ladies and gentlemen of New York, there is no difference between slavery and polygamy. I agree with Ann, but I will take it one step further. Both women, black and white, work incessantly; are repeatedly raped, sodomized, and loaned out to other men; and must have as many babies as their husbands or masters desire. And if they disobey and rebel, they are mutilated, killed, or exiled."

The faces of the people in the audience went ashen from shock. Harriet spoke it as she saw it, which made her a very effective and persuasive speaker.

It was Katryn's turn to speak. Everyone eagerly awaited her point of view since she did not practice polygamy.

But, seeing the restlessness growing among the audience, Bishop Terrance decided to call for a ten-minute intermission.

The church woman had baked oatmeal raisin cookies and a big lemon sheet cake with lemon icing—made from several round cakes pieced together—to serve with lemonade and raspberry tea. Bishop Terrance thought the debate had come to an opportune breaking point and wanted to put some time between Harriet's and Katryn's answers. He knew there could be excitement from the audience and anger among the contestants, and he wanted to avoid both by weakening their emotions.

Katryn and Harriet met in the hallway and just chuckled at each other.

"I can't wait to hear your answer to the last question, Katryn."

"Well, Harriet, you will just have to wait. I have a good reply; it comes from my heart. No matter how this debate ends, I would love to invite you for afternoon tea tomorrow in my suite at four o'clock at the Plaza."

"You're on, little lady!" replied Harriet with a warlike chant.

Bishop Terrance called upon Katryn to answer, but first, he thanked the audience for their patience, self-discipline, and good behavior. He was actually talking about their restraint from criticizing the contestants by throwing beer bottles at them and spitting in their faces. Even the Sacred Four Hundred succumbed to such vulgar behavior at times.

Katryn answered, "I have searched my soul and can say without a doubt that I have not personally experienced any of the evils of slavery that are taking place in the medieval South. So, my answer is an unequivocal no. You can't compare apples and beans! Hence, there is no similarity between slavery and polygamy, and I rest my case. I rest my case. But there are other issues I wish to discuss, although I can't get into them tonight. I have heard rumors of unhappy sister wives. So, when I return to Utah Territory, I plan on solving them in an intelligent and fair manner."

Katryn sounded confident and very determined to help these pitiful "desperate housewives" from the mid-to-late nineteenth century.

Bishop Terrance said, "Thank you, ladies," and continued with the next question. "Question number five: What is the purpose of polygamy?"

Harriet replied, "To keep women barefoot and pregnant. Mormon men see women as slaves in the form of baby-making machines, always doing their bidding without respect and love."

The audience roared and clapped. Some rednecks from Alabama waved the Confederate flag and loudly booed.

Katryn said, "The purpose of polygamy is to practice the principle of plural marriage and get sealed for all eternity. Also, it allows men to become a god over their own planet—the height the men can reach in celestial heaven depends on how many children they produce and the degree of their righteousness. Some men may become gods, but so far, no one has."."

You could have heard a pin drop! Everyone was in shock, with many mouths open wide in disbelief to the words they'd just heard.

Ann replied, "I agree with Katryn. Sealing is a big part of the purpose. If we keep the principle of plural marriage, God will bestow many blessings and keep us together for all eternity."

You could tell the audience was perplexed, but they kept vigilant and focused until the end of the debate.

Bishop Terrance uttered with a red face, "Very interesting, ladies." After a moment, he said, "Question number six: Describe what Mormon living means to you."

Katryn replied, "Being a Mormon for me means sacrificing my

personal goal, to get an education, for my loved ones' needs; spreading the gospel in the Women's Relief Society; and loving and serving God, my husband, and our family before all others, and my country."

Ann said, "Being a Mormon for me is difficult because I am not the pretty one. Sister Ruth is very beautiful. My intelligence is far above my husband's. I don't make him feel special.. After my sister's wives were added, I only saw my husband for supper, so I was lonely. My strong testimony of the gospel got me through those sad times. The truth is, I just don't like sharing my marriage bed with anyone, even though my husband promised to love and cherish me for all eternity. Hogwash! I wish I could elaborate, but I must remain ladylike."

Harriet answered, "Let me be perfectly clear: I am not, never was, and never will be a damn Mormon. Thus I have a single Mormon experience to recount."

Bishop Terrance said, "Astonishing responses, ladies. Just astonishing!" Then he asked question number seven: "Aren't religious beliefs like polygamy protected by the United States Constitution?"

Harriet answered, "Unfortunately, yes, and fortunately, no. The law of the land doesn't always get followed properly. Sometimes bad things happen for good reasons. As the Mormons birthed more children, they became a threat to the Gentiles' way of life since they voted the way Brigham Young dictated them to vote, which resulted in a very powerful large bloc of power. As many saw the writing on the wall, the Mormons were pushed out of several states until they could take no more indignation and cruelty; they left their country, which was supposed to honor and protect their religious rights but chose not to because of fear, speculation, and greed."

Katryn replied, "So true, but you know there is a lot of corruption in government, especially since the Civil War. Representation in Congress hasn't been the best! There is an old saying: 'Money talks and polygamy walks—right out of the United States and into Mexico and Canada.'"

Ann said, "I love our United States Constitution because it protects our religious freedoms, but somehow the people of Missouri and Illinois are suffering from illiteracy, prejudice, and greed. They kicked us out, confiscated our money and property, raped our women, and killed many men, women, and children during the Haun's Mill Massacre."

Bishop Terrance said, "Ladies, shocking answers that have opened up a brave new world of existential thought!". He thanked the audience for their patience, adding that he hoped they were enjoying the debate. "There is just one more question left, one I hope will solve a mystery. Question number eight: If polygamy is banned, how should plural wives and their children be incorporated back into society without their husbands, belongings, and financial support?"

Ann replied, "I hate to see the families divided, but with that said, I feel wives should be expected to own their own homes, live with their children, and receive an annuity for life from the culprit who broke the families up, namely, the United States."

Harriet answered, "I can see a need for the United States government to offer assistance, but not as elaborate as individual homes. I tend to support group homes where there would be tons of comradeship and shared separation anxiety. Not every woman wants to leave polygamy and break up her family. Then after a period, each family could live on their own if they so choose at our government's expense. After all, free slaves were issued forty acres and a mule! Furthermore, these women deserve some compensation for being forced out of their homes and left penniless!"

The audience went wild, screaming, cheering, and raising their fists, while Bishop Terrance banged his gavel many times to quiet them, but to no avail. Some started to march around the room, chanting, "Viva La Stowe."

Bishop Terrance had no choice. He whipped out his pistol and shot in the air and demanded the crowd leave or return to their seats. All of a sudden, you could have heard a pin drop. The debate continued.

Katryn said, "I will not leave my family even though it would be the law. We will all move to Mexico or Canada, where Mormons can practice our religion and promote the principle of plural marriage. This is what God has asked from all of us."

Bishop Terrance thanked all the contestants and the audience for participating in this unique debate. Then he moved to announce the winner of the debate.

"Ladies and gentlemen and contestants, I asked some powerful questions tonight, and all these ladies stepped up to the plate and responded very well. Thank you, ladies, for a fine job. But unfortunately, we can only have one winner. So, I am going to ask everyone in the audience to clap for your choice. The contestant with the most applause will win the prize."

The audience stood and applauded and cheered. Everyone knew Katryn's husband didn't practice polygamy, so she welcomed the opportunity to explain the pros and cons of the principle. Having been raised Jewish, she knew the Old Testament inside and out. She proved quite the competitor to Brigham Young's nineteenth wife, Ann, and to author and activist Harriet Beecher Stowe. Her answers blew the audience away.

She used vocabulary they had never heard before; she made them think outside the box and heightened their interest in Mormonism. Stowe came in as a strong second, and Ann was third.

Katryn's parents were so happy to hear their daughter would move to uphold her beliefs. Perhaps she and her family would move closer to New York. Possibly Rhode Island, the duchess pondered, and she and the duke could travel up there to see them on their yacht, the Oleander She and the duke could travel up there to see them on their yacht, the *Oleander*.

"Duke, darling, you must encourage our daughter to move closer. I can tell she is going to need our support once she returns to the Utah Territory and Thomas, her beloved, marries his fourth wife even though he promised her he never would. He is very righteous in his religious beliefs, and he is outnumbered by hundreds of polygamous men. We need to be there for our daughter and our grandchildren," the duchess said.

"Darling, I have it under control. You can count on me to help in any way to get our little princess back home. But we must help her secretly move those abused Mormon slaves to a safer place where they can regain their dignity and self-respect. Perhaps with our effort, she will find her way home to New York," Katryn's father said.

Katryn walked up to her parents. "Well, Dad, what did you think of the debate?"

"One thing for sure, you certainly deserved to win. Your answers were the most informative and mind-boggling. Can I have some of that delicious-looking candy, Daughter?"

"Yes, of course. And, Mother, may I please have the bubble bath and powder?"

"I don't think the audience ever heard of plural marriage and becoming a god in the manner you described it, dear. The people sitting near us just gasped when you mentioned how a Mormon husband could become a god by having more children and wives and being righteous. You must give me some books so I can read more about these religious beliefs," the duchess said. "That religion just intrigues me. How the Mormons have survived all these years on faith and hard work—simply amazing!"

"I invited Harriet for tea tomorrow at four o'clock, Father, so we can discuss saving those women and using our railroad car to sneak them away to San Francisco, preferably to the Palace Hotel first and then beyond to Los Angeles. Oh, Father, could you ask Jonathan to join us? We will need his input on how the hotel could help the ladies."

"Consider it done, my little princess," the duke said.

The meeting was very successful, and all participants expressed fidelity to the purpose and promised to help in any way to free all oppressed women who wanted to escape polygamy. Afterward, standing on the wooden platform at the train station, Katryn kissed her parents goodbye, boarded Wellington's railroad car, and headed back to Utah Territory. Katryn knew she was going to persuade her friends to assist in her cause. She had stayed up all night prior to the meeting, writing plans for her new project. First, she would get her most sympathetic and trusted friends in the Relief Society to help identify abused Mormon women in the St. George area. Then the search would be expanded to Salt Lake until the entire Utah Territory had been plucked of unhappy, abused wives looking for an alternative life in California. It was a wonderful project that ultimately became very successful, especially after Brigham Young died in 1877 from appendicitis.

Katryn knew that the dreaded day was coming when Thomas would ask her if he could take a fourth wife—since his first two had died and he wanted more children than she could give him—and she would say no and walk away before she gave in to his pouting ways by hanging his lovely head down and sighing as if he were going to cry.

"I did not sign up for plural marriage in my heart," Katryn would say to her beloved in a recurring dream after he asked her for another wife. "You must do what you need to do—and so do I—to stay in this marriage. I will leave you and take our children and go back to New York if you marry another. Please open your eyes. My womb is open; I can still conceive and give you more missionaries for the Lord. Don't be unreasonable and greedy. Please, Thomas, don't impose such mental cruelty upon me. I am not ready to be replaced." She would say this over and over in her recurring dream. Then in these dreams, Thomas would hold Katryn in his strong muscled arms and kiss her. He would always tell her not to worry, and then she would awake.

When the day finally came, of course Katryn got very upset. She cried and stamped her feet.

"You are my true love, my beautiful wife, but Brigham has asked me to take more wives. Please understand that he has commissioned me and my father to move south to northern Arizona to assist in repairing this one stubborn dam that will not remain standing. The dam breaks after two days; tons of water are wasted, and livestock and families go without water for days. Not a good beginning for a new Mormon settlement, my love."

"I knew this day was coming, but I just can't condone sharing you, Thomas. You and I are different, but our love will sustain anything. We have a connection. I'll just die if I see you kiss another wife," Katryn responded. "Please, I'm begging you, don't destroy our great love."

"Katryn, you will live. Furthermore, we must follow the Prophet's wishes, or we will be excommunicated or killed by the Danites. The Prophet means business; he doesn't fool around. Brigham wants to see results. John Bushman took a second wife, whom he took to St. Joseph, Arizona—now called Joseph City. He left his first wife in Orem to tend the farm and care for their children. So, I could do a similar thing. If you have more children and the fourth wife has many children, I think Brigham will be pleased and satisfied. You can join us once we are settled, darling, just like John's first wife did."

"Who is she? I know you have a wife picked out, or else the subject would never have come up."

"Darling, if it weren't for the Prophet, the thought of a new wife would never enter my head. I love you above God and my church. You are the devil's daughter, always tempting me with your inviting smile. Please don't worry, darling. I hear in order to become a state, Utah must be free of polygamy. Also, the men are already looking for a candidate to replace Brigham. He is an invalid now and stays close to home. He didn't even attend John D. Lee's execution. You know John was his adopted son. Please, please don't worry, my darling. Forgive me for bringing the whole matter up about another wife. I sometimes get confused when I think of what Brigham asked of me one day five years ago."

"No, I did not know that, Thomas. Well, I guess the Prophet had some good in him to adopt a homeless orphan. Also, I know he started two small colleges, one in Salt Lake and one in Provo, which shows he cares about education and our youth's future," Katryn said. "Remember, my father drummed education down my throat, and I was sent away to finish school in Lancaster, Pennsylvania, where I learned about many fascinating countries I would love to visit. I spoke French fluently and read the classics; I especially loved to read Voltaire, who talks about freedom. Since I have been here in Utah Territory, there has been no time to enjoy a moment of reading. You, our children, and the Relief Society have come first."

"Now that you are back, my little darling, I will ensure you have time for a bubble bath and your Voltaire. By the way, Wife, should I be jealous of a Frenchman?" he asked with a smile.

"Oh, Thomas, that sounds wonderful. I could use some domestic help. I have a huge project that just came to the forefront for the Relief Society and, I will tell you about it sometime soon. But for now, I just want to take a bubble bath, soak, and read."

"And I, my sweet wife, will soak along with you and listen to the words of Mr. Voltaire."

With that remark, Thomas and Katryn got reacquainted after a month of abstinence, and the honeymoon started all over again. They even took time to visit the waterfall where they had made covenants to each other never to take another lover or spouse. Thomas knew that Brigham didn't have long, but he did have to live in Arizona for a spell to fix the dam. And he knew Katryn's work at home and with the Relief Society would keep her in St. George. But that spiritual need to take more wives and propagate more children was ingrained in him. Secretly he knew he couldn't refuse the Prophet's command even after Brigham passed away.

CHAPTER 19
HUNTING FOR ELK

One day during the fall, Thomas said goodbye to Katryn. He was going hunting for elk.

"See you when I see you. I want you and the children to have plenty to eat while I'm away in Arizona. That dam in St. Joseph's will take about six months to repair. I am going to hate every minute we are apart. I will be staying with John Bushman and his family. I will write you every night, my darling."

"Thomas, I put together a little care basket with venison jerky, apricot jam, oatmeal raisin cookies, clean underwear for a week, and three pairs of pants with matching plaid shirts. I also packed your Book of Mormon and our family Christmas picture to keep you warm at night with our smiles. When you send me a letter with a return address, I can replenish everything," Katryn said.

"Honey, I will be back tonight with an elk. Make some mashed potatoes and gravy. I want my favorite meal before I head south without my favorite gal. I know we have some elk from last hunting season hanging in the storage room. I will be leaving in three days. Surprise me, darling. Be adventurous," he hinted. "You and the children can visit me in Arizona just before I return home. I think traveling and meeting people is a wonderful way to educate children. It will be like a huge long camping trip back to civilization."

Katryn thought that Arizona must be very primitive, with no bathhouses or general stores. *Thomas sure has his work cut out for him. I understand there isn't even a ward or temple yet; the saints meet for Sunday services under a tent in a field of purple sage. So glad we are not all joining Thomas now; I don't do primitive very well.* She chuckled to herself.

In attendance at the meeting with Brigham Young, two days prior to Thomas's leaving for Arizona were Miles Romney, Martin and

Thomas Huntzmon, Martin Bozemon, John Lee, John Allen, John Bushman, and Sam Udall.

The tree leaves bristled as the horses pulling the carriage galloped down the pink cobbled street toward Brigham Young's winter home, as it was called in St. George. The wind was strong, turning over flowerpots filled with geraniums in front of the Prophet's orange brick home with green trim, while six men sat upright on smooth black leather chairs, anticipating the meeting with their Prophet. He'd sent a telegram to each one asking them to drop everything and meet him at once to discuss matters of great importance regarding the church's future.

As the carriage pulled up to the entrance, Brigham was prancing back and forth in his dark-stained-oak-paneled office, waiting for his special team to arrive. When the carriage pulled in front of the mansion, he ran out to greet them.

"Brothers, thank you for coming on short notice; there is much to discuss of grave importance. Franklin will show you to your rooms while Matilda will prepare some yeast rolls, cold pheasant, and German potato salad with pears and goat cheese for dessert. I made some tasty apple cider to quench your thirst. Wait until you see the beautiful down quilts on your beds that some of my wives have made over the years. They will keep you warm and toasty this fall evening. After dinner, we will retire to my library, shoot some billiards, drink some of my homemade wine, and smoke fine Cuban cigars while discussing a very delicate pressing matter—the preservation of polygamy," Brigham elaborated.

All the men looked at each other in amazement in response to what the Prophet had just said they would be doing after dinner.

"Okay, who wants to challenge me first at billiards?" Brigham asked.

"I would be honored to take up such a challenge," said Miles Romney.

"So be it," the Prophet said. "Let's flip to see who is going first.

Here's a Gold Eagle coin, Brother Bozemon. You flip."

Brigham was a big man, tall, broad in the shoulders, and well-muscled in his arms and legs. But he did manage to sweat a bit after he hit the white ball hit the ten ball hit the eight ball, which put the seven ball in the far right pocket. He took his pool cue and once again hit the white ball and missed.

"Oh well, got to leave some for you, Brother Romney." The Prophet chuckled.

Throughout the next six games, Brigham discussed polygamy and challenged the men to help save the practice by moving their families to Arizona and then to Mexico and marrying more wives.

"In order to become a state, I am afraid we will have to give up polygamy—at least for five years. My plan is to bring it back once we are entitled to two senators and several representatives; they will write laws to overturn the abominable manifesto that is coming. But until that time comes, expanding our colony to other areas will continue at a fast pace. Brother Card will move to Canada, where polygamy is not a bad word and is not forbidden. Canada needs strong large families to help cultivate its vast fertile lands and grow its population. And we will provide that for Her Majesty.

"Brothers Romney, Bushman, Huntzmon, Lee, Bozemon, Allen, and Udall will settle in northern Arizona by the Little Colorado River and the White Mountains. Men, we need dams built to hold water for domestic and agricultural purposes. The few families that have been trying to survive down there have complained of not having anyone who knows how to build a dam that doesn't fall apart. There is also another challenge—rustlers stealing livestock. Here is where the Huntzmons and Bozemons can help. They can shoot straight and have served in the Nauvoo and Mormon Battalion for many years. Managing rustlers would be an easy accomplishment for them."

"Prophet, you can't mean that about taking more wives," said Brother Bozemon.

"Yes, I do. The Lord has spoken to me in a vision. His message was to take more wives and multiply. And remember, God will bless you tenfold if you follow the principle of plural marriage. Are there any questions? Yes, Brother Romney?"

Miles Romney stood six feet tall with brown hair and green eyes—a very handsome man. He was righteous and a faithful believer in the principle. "Just how many wives is that, Prophet?" he asked.

"Well, if you sire seventy-eight children, then you will need at least ten wives, which is seven or eight children per wife. And remember, they will not all get along at first, but they will appreciate sharing mundane chores like washing, hanging, ironing, and folding clothes. Most wives love to cook and bake, so they will need their own homes with huge kitchens. Oh! How funny it is to hear them fight! Am I right, brothers?"

The men chuckled and laughed and shook their heads affirmatively.

"And one more thing!" Brigham proclaimed. "If you have a favorite wife, for heaven's sake, don't show it. That is where I made my mistake with Amelia. Eleven wives have divorced me, and it hurts my feelings to have failed to please them, but I am older now and an invalid, so I let them go."

Thomas looked at his dad in shock; he shook his head and raised his shoulders. Martin knew what he was thinking. Both Katryn and Esther frowned on plural marriage. They both had had their husbands to themselves throughout their marriages so far. But soon, their lives were going to be dramatically changed forever if their husbands were to marry more wives.

"Kind of scary, Dad. Katryn will leave me like she said one too many times. If I marry another wife, she will move back to New York with our children."

Martin just stared at his son and said, "I am in a similar situation. Your mother just hates anyone else using her kitchen. And another woman using me for sex, well, that won't work at all. She would surely leave me. God knows where she would go. I love your mother and would die without her yeast biscuits and compassionate heart."

"Yeah, Katryn makes the best brisket in St. George with cherry pie. I love her, Dad. What are we going to do?"

"God will show us the way, Son. Don't you worry."

Martin and Thomas just shrugged their shoulders and drank more of Brigham's homemade wine—the reserve stock he didn't sell in his stores.

The next day the carriage left at 6:00 a.m. sharp. The men had a lot to think about. Suddenly Thomas yelled out, "Stop the carriage! I must puke. The wine that the Prophet gave us was bad."

"That was not alcohol but a putrid imitation to make us sick, so we will never touch the stuff when we are down in Arizona and Mexico. But those cigars were real," John D. Lee said.

"Every time I think of how they smell; I want to upchuck everything in my stomach. The Prophet surely knows how to prepare his men for temptation," Martin Bozemon uttered.

"Yes, he does! We are so lucky he's on our side. I helped Father make that fake wine so you would get sick. Sorry, fellas, but I was following orders," John D. confessed.

On the way back to Cedar City, Thomas asked the brothers who were successfully living the principle how they had persuaded their first wives to accept more wives.

"Well, it is never a smooth transition for the last wife to accept the newest one. It is sort of like the pecking order with horses. It usually works out after time passes, and the women become friends and need each other's help," answered Brother Romney.

"You definitely have to have a bedroom schedule. I always take Sundays for myself to replenish my manhood," replied Brother

Udall.

"And the bigger the house, the better—or build each wife her own home," touted John Bushman.

John D. Lee shouted, "Only a rich Mormon could build each wife her own home. Since Brigham commissioned me to run the ferry at the Little Colorado River in northern Arizona in 1857, I have made a fortune and have several wives and houses. He gave me Emma Louise Batchelor the day after Mountain Meadows as a reward for carrying out his orders. And since she is so pretty and loving, she has her own home."

The men just rolled their eyes at him and half-heartedly shook their heads in disbelief.

"Good for you, John. I can't think of a more deserving fellow to obtain such a commission," said John Bushman. "I know of your wife, Emma; she has healing powers like my mother, Elizabeth Degen Bushman. They both birthed over a hundred breech babies, and those babies all lived."

"For your information, my first home in Arizona was only a one-room building with a stairway leading to the second floor until more rooms could be added," John D. said. "It was crowded, but we managed. Then I built more homes for my other wives as I became richer."

"John D., where can we stay when we arrive?" asked Brother Romney.

"You can pitch tents and put your horses in my big barn. You can wash up at my home and eat with us. There is plenty of wild game and fish at Mormon Lake."

"Sounds inviting, John D. Thank you for your generosity," Thomas said.

The rest of the men thanked John D. and shook his hand.

One of the most annoying things about starting over in a new wilderness was determining where to sleep, eat, wash, and secure your horses. But the men were lucky; all their bases were covered at Lee's Ferry.

After a few years in northern Arizona, the Bushmans lived in Joseph City, formerly St. Joseph's, and built strong, lasting dams; the Udalls and the Huntzmons started cattle ranches south of Holbrook; Miles Romney settled a town called Taylor; and William Jordon Flake settled a town named after him and Erastus Snow called Snowflake. This area became very busy after the railroad was built and coal was discovered. In 1890, the Mormons outlawed polygamy, as had the United States, so Utah became a state. Chaos ensued, but polygamy openly continued in Canada and Mexico thanks to the astute strategies of Brigham Young. Secretly, polygamy continued in Utah and Arizona. The brothers did not want to break up their families; they didn't want any other man to raise their children or sleep with their wives. After all, God doesn't make mistakes. They firmly believed God wanted polygamy to prosper, and so it did after 1890, openly in Mexico and Canada but secretly in Utah.

CHAPTER 20
GIDDY MADSEN AND THE FREEDOM TRIAL

Early 1850

On a night smelling sweet from cherry blossoms, during a Salt Lake City Relief Society meeting, a black slave, Sister Giddy Madsen from Mississippi, walked in with one of Brigham Young's frustrated concubines named Sidney. As the story went on, Giddy was thirteen and pregnant. She claimed someone raped her, impregnated her, and left her on the Prophet's doorstep. She wouldn't say who'd done it. One of Brigham's bodyguards, Clinton, found her bloody body outside on the front porch, hunched over a pool of blood. He gently carried her tiny protruding body inside the mansion. One look at her stomach, and Brigham Young decided to make Giddy his responsibility until the baby was born., she could decide her fate, but the baby stayed. But Giddy chose to leave before little Rachel was born; she was determined her offspring would grow up free from slavery. She wanted a better life for her child without complications. There were so many Mormon secrets, so many church rituals, that she was afraid to comprehend the whys behind them. And church practices such as blood atonement, plural marriage, celestial heaven, forcing thirteen-year-old girls to marry much older men, and not letting blacks into the priesthood puzzled her. But now Giddy was presented with an opportunity to escape. The time was right; the birth was in two months—time to make her move. One of Brigham's concubines wanted out from under his plutocratic leadership. Miss Sidney, who'd heard of California being a free state for blacks, figured it would be free for white women also. To her, being a polygamous wife was the same as being a black slave. She felt Mormon women had no voice; they were just chattel to their husbands with an accompanying number—wife no. 4, etc.

Luckily for Giddy, Colonel Richard Smith, a new church converts from Mississippi, had been commissioned by Brigham Young to start a new Mormon mission in San Bernardino, California. These two women went along to guard the sheep and cattle—something Giddy was known to be an expert at, in addition to birthing babies. She also knew how to cure most ailments with herbs, so Colonel Smith was happy to have her along.

The date was September 11, 1851, six years before the Mountain Meadows Massacre had occurred. Colonel Smith led his new congregation over the California Trail and camped in Mountain Meadows, thirty miles southeast of Cedar City. They were tired and needed nourishment, and the animals needed to rest. Giddy, Sidney, and a young boy named Jacob tended to the livestock. One of the colonel's horses had a sour foot, and only Giddy knew how to fix it with a poultice of fresh green herbs she had gathered from the surrounding lush woodlands.

"Miss Giddy," the inquisitive light-brown-skinned Mexican boy murmured, "this meadow gives me the shivers. And the wind is howling like it is speaking a foreboding message: 'Beware, murder is near.'"

"I hear it too, Jacob," Giddy said, "but it says something bad will happen here. We'd better leave this area quickly. I have come too close to freedom to lose it now."

"Miss Sidney, how come you don't say anything?" the boy asked.

"Too afraid, I guess. I believe you two, but I don't know what the wind is saying. It is just blowing loud and strong, and it frightens me," Sidney remarked.

"I'll tell the colonel to leave early in the morning because there's a big storm coming. He'd never believe my mystical powers," Giddy said.

As the wagon train closed camp and pulled out, and started for

California, Giddy had a vision that made her blood curdle. She saw naked and eaten bodies of men, women, and children slaughtered there in the name of God knows what—Mormon revenge under the subterfuge of blood atonement, the vision told her.

"Miss Giddy, do you smell something sour?" Jacob asked.

Giddy responded, "I smell something, but I can't seem to place it. Maybe a dead cow or wild bear. It is rank, I agree. But this will pass. In two days, we will be in San Bernardino, where you will smell orange blossoms all day long, I promise."

The wagon train trekked forward toward their destination at the speed of a tortoise. It took them an extra day because of a dust storm, but they arrived in San Bernardino safe and sound. Giddy and her two helpers took the cattle and sheep to the livery stables to eat and rest. Tired as they were, the three musketeers made a beeline for the general store, where the restrooms were located for travelers, while the others replenished their wagons. There they would find a sink to wash up and an indoor toilet. Giddy thought she had gone to heaven, although the Prophet's mansion had indoor plumbing, which she used.

"Gosh, isn't this nice, Sidney, an indoor bathroom with a deep sink to bathe in? Thank you, Jesus," Giddy exclaimed.

"When we are finished, Giddy, let's find a place to eat. I want a big juicy steak with thin fried round potatoes and Mexican beans, a large eight-ounce glass of milk and a cinnamon roll with melted butter just dripping off onto my plate," Sidney exclaimed with hunger in her green eyes.

As the trio walked into the San Bernardino Hotel, they sat next to a table where a distinguished couple was sitting and eating their supper. They appeared to be without their master, but they were so dignified and polite and dressed in expensive white gentlemen's and ladies' clothing that Giddy could tell they were well taken care of. Giddy heard the woman say something to her.

"Would you like to join our table? Our treat! I'm Sally, and this is my husband, Jim Owens, originally from Virginia. We own a ranch just to the south of town, about three thousand acres. We raise sheep and Hereford cattle where there are green hills where they all graze peacefully. Also, we raise horses for the army."

Giddy's mouth dropped open; you could see her tongue hanging out. Her eyes were glassy, and her breathing was rapid. Suddenly she jumped out of her seat and cheered. "My name is Giddy, and the Lord must live in California. How do I get me a ranch?" she asked the Owenses.

"Gee, you are getting ahead of yourself, girl. Tell us about yourself first, like where you came from and why you are here sitting across from us," Sally said.

"Well, I was born in North Carolina, got separated from my parents when I was ten and was sold to a Mr. Jeffers from Texas. He joined the Mormon Church and moved us to the Utah Territory. His overseer, Jeb, raped me. When I became pregnant, he dropped me off in front of the Prophet Brigham Young's mansion in Salt Lake. He didn't want Mr. Jeffers to know, or he would have been fired. Mr. Jeffers is very strict about chastity, being Mormon and all," Giddy said.

"Oh, you poor dear," Sally uttered. "Please go on."

"Then I lived in the Prophet's home along with some of his wives. One evening Miss Sidney was going to attend a Relief Society meeting and asked me to join her. I did, and here we are. A week later, we hitched a ride with Colonel Smith's wagon train headed for San Bernardino as ranch hands driving the cattle and sheep forward, feeding and watering them along the way, and tending to them when we arrived until they could be put out to green pasture," Giddy added.

"You know, Giddy, California is a free state. There are no slaves here—slavery is forbidden. Anyone caught owning slaves goes to jail for ninety days. You and your friends are welcome at our ranch for as long as you like," Jim declared. "Let me ask you a question. Do you girls have any nursing skills?"

"I do," Giddy answered. "I can birth babies, sew up wounds, and break a fever, and I can use all sorts of herbs and potions to cure infections and snakebites."

"Well, Giddy, I have some good news for you. Nurses are at a premium here in California; they make thirty dollars a month, and they work round the clock some days. You can work as many shifts as you can stand and make extra money. I know one nurse who invested her money by purchasing lots in a new thriving town called Los Angeles—City of Angels. She plans to be rich one day. As a matter of fact, she is one of us, a former slave called Biddy Mason. Her master became a Mormon too, and she was brought out here to California to be his slave, but she had other plans. She went to court and won her freedom. Now Biddy is working as a private nurse somewhere in Los Angeles and is still buying up lots. I bet she will become a millionaire one day. Biddy used to stay with Jim and me, and she saved every penny she ever made for her future family. She always said she wanted her offspring to have the best education money could buy, live in fancy homes, wear fine clothes, and ride in elegant carriages drawn by the prettiest horses. She is very religious. I bet one day she will contribute a lot of money to some church she will start. Biddy is one powerful and determined American woman. When she puts her mind to doing something, she masters it. Take tennis, for instance; she won three church championships. Her speed and sure-footedness gave her an edge over her opponents. Even some men couldn't beat her backhand. See, hard work can get you anything your heart desires. So don't ever give up, ladies," Jim said.

Sidney's purpose for having made the trip was to find a husband in San Francisco. She had a soprano operatic voice, beautiful long red hair, and a very small waist—three prerequisites to catching a rich husband. She landed a job working in a high-class restaurant singing songs from *La Boehme*. One day her prince walked in and carried her off to his castle in Bavaria.

Giddy stayed with the Owenses until she moved to Los Angeles, where she started a nursing home for the elderly and did quite well. She joined the First Methodist Episcopalian African American Church of Los Angeles. One day she met its founder, Biddy Mason, and told her how pleased she was to finally meet her idol. Giddy told her that the Owenses had a plaque outside her old bedroom door: Biddy Mason Slept Here! Biddy just smiled and ushered Giddy inside and quickly pointed out the collection box. *Some things never change,* Giddy thought. And so, the southern Freedom Trail began until Katryn Klein Wellington Huntzmon reorganized it to help Mormon wives escape polygamy in the late 1870s. In fact, her California contact was none other than Biddy Mason.

CHAPTER 21
THE UNDERGROUND MORMON RAILROAD

During the late 1800s, plural wives from Utah Territory who wanted to escape jail time for having been a polygamous wives before the 1890s sought refuge with Katryn and boarded the train, and headed west to San Francisco's Palace Hotel. Sometimes—not frequently, but occasionally—there were Mormon wives who were deeply fond of each other and wanted to live together for the rest of their lives. They held hands, shared kisses and embraces, and wanted to take their relationship to the next level—freedom to love whom they desired and out in the open. They also brought their children with them and sought country property, where they made goat cheese and cashmere yarn. The shorn coats of three to five goats made one sweater. These were two sought-after and cherished items that people would pay top dollar for.

Education for women in the 1800s among Mormon leaders was taboo. Brigham Young was illiterate and saw no need for women to have an education. He felt the only learning women needed was to learn how to cook and bake, play the piano or violin, and tend to a garden and grow vegetables. It was a huge plus if his wives could sing. Cultured Mormon wives were a rarity. That is why he favored his wife, Amelia, for her piano skills and her ability to sing his favorite German song. All he wanted to do for his women, it appeared, was keep them barefoot and pregnant. He saw them as baby-making factories for the church, turning out nine to eighteen bundles of joy in their lifetimes. Brigham had fifty-five wives and fifty-seven children from sixteen of his wives. He had an overabundance of love to share with his children. But for some of his wives, affection was a different story. He felt they were too needy.

Life was difficult for many of the wives who did not buy into polygamy. They did buy into staying married and having babies so they would get into celestial heaven. Their biggest hurt was watching their husband pay amorous attention to his new wife and shower her with more elaborate gifts than he'd given them. Depression and suicide were not uncommon among sister wives. These women hadn't been brought up to share their husbands, give up privacy in the bedroom, and sacrifice all for the family, while certain favored wives had it all: fancy dresses, furs, hats, satin shoes, leather boots, their carriage, and a huge weekly allowance. Brigham's favorite wife, Amelia, traveled abroad and just sent him the bills.

Most Mormon wives accepted their station in life as a path to salvation and knew sacrifices here on earth put them and their husbands at a higher level in celestial heaven. But on the other hand, some wives had who had had enough heartbreak and wanted out. They dreamed of being free and had heard of Katryn's underground railroad that helped oppressed and disillusioned polygamist wives escape their miserable lives of white slavery. They wanted a chance to live like Amelia Young did—cultured, educated, and financially independent. Most of these wives were under thirty and desired a new marriage, one where they didn't have to share husbands, bedrooms, and kitchens. They all possessed midwifery skills, which were in high demand in California. They knew they could become wealthy if they invested some money into buying lots in San Francisco and purchasing shares in the California Pacific Railroad.

Some young Mormon sons also preferred to follow the beat of their drums, dress in women's clothing, and sing on stage. One evening when Katryn was presiding over a quilting class, a young woman of about thirty-five and her fourteen-year-old son approached her.

"Sister Huntzmon, may I speak with you after class?"

"Of course. Please meet me in my office, which is down the hall in room ten. It would be my pleasure to assist you, Sister Young, in any way possible," Katryn said. "I will be there in ten minutes. Let me just get the ladies started."

Turning to the group, Katryn said, "May I have your attention, sisters? Tonight, we are going to tie this beautiful wedding quilt, which will go to Sister Jameson for her wedding night. I just need four volunteers to take each end and form a rectangle. Then we need four more ladies to tie the front and back together. Thank you, Sisters Smith, Dunn, Griffiths, and Davis, for volunteering. Okay, the rest of you ladies, please start tying." Voilà, in twenty minutes, the quilt was ready. "Great job, sisters! See you all on Sunday."

As Katryn hurried down to her office, she asked herself why one of Brigham's wives would desire to speak with her here, at the chapel, of all places. *Usually, a wife of the Prophet has me visit her at the Lion House for privacy. Please guide me, Lord, so I can advise appropriately.* The office door opened.

"Sister Huntzmon, may I present my son, Clarence G. Young, sixteen years old and already an accomplished pianist and opera singer."

"How do you do, Brother Young? It is a pleasure to meet any son of the Prophet," Katryn said.

"His father wants him to run his general store in Salt Lake. My son has more to offer the world than keeping books on tools, groceries, building materials, yarn, and cloth. Oh, and let's not forget the wine his father makes to sell to the Gentiles."

All three broke out into laughter. Mormons weren't supposed to know about the wine.

"Clarence would like to pursue his dream to entertain people with his musical gifts."

"Is this true, Clarence?"
"Yes, Sister Huntzmon; it is my dream."

Katryn took a deep breath. She knew she was going to have to expose the secrets of the Western Underground Railroad to San Francisco.

"How may I be of service, Sister Young?"

Now it was Sister Young's turn to take a deep breath. She was about to be brazen as a wild goat.

"There is a rumor, sister, that you help women escape from polygamy on the train going to San Francisco. Well, I came here tonight to book a passage on that train for Clarence and me. I hear it leaves at midnight. Then after a short time, only I will return to my mundane existence. But first I must settle my son in California, where he will be free to live the life he desires—as a classical opera singer."

"This is how it works, Sister Young: You and Clarence will arrive at the station at eleven thirty. You will stay in my father's private club car, where all your personal needs will be accommodated by a woman named Bertie, a former slave. She will be waiting for you at the station. The train will take nine hours to reach San Francisco. Then you will be met by a yellow and black carriage, which will take you and your son to the most extravagant and opulent hotel in the world—the Palace Hotel. A gentleman called Hubert will help your son find lodging, education, and employment. Perhaps the hotel has a show he can perform in. If not, Hubert will find one that does. You will be in good hands. Good luck!" Katryn said.

'That sounds perfect. How can I ever repay you, Sister Huntzmon?"

"Don't worry about that now," Katryn replied. "My true reward comes each time I help someone escape polygamy and, in this case, achieve musical justice. But my causes do need donations. Perhaps you can find a way to get the Prophet to donate without knowing, or some of your women friends who are in the same circumstance—a secret fundraiser during afternoon tea, perhaps? I love that this movement liberates women caught in white slavery; it has purpose, dignity, and justice," exclaimed Katryn.

A few years later, one of Brigham Young's sons, Brigham Morris Young, did three missions in Hawaii, two while he was single and one after he was married with children. He must have observed the Japanese art of cross-dressing, called *Otokonoko,* while he was there. Cross-dressing was the rage in Japan, a work of art where men sang while wearing women's wigs, makeup, silk floral dresses, and button-up black leather boots. In Japan, a cross-dresser was respected and regarded with much admiration for their acting and singing skills. But here in the United States, cross-dressers were belittled and ridiculed. Being a cross-dresser didn't preclude desiring the same sex for amorous affection. In the theater world, they were mere entertainers on a stage, nothing more, nothing less. When Morris Young returned to Utah Territory after his third mission, he spent five years on stage singing as a cross-dresser, impersonating an Italian singer from 1885 to 1890 called Madam Pattirini. It was said that no one recognized him. His family was very supportive and loved to watch him perform. He also became very prominent in the Mormon Church; through his father's inspiration, he started the Young Men's Association for Mutual Improvement. Morris was happily married to his wife, Celestia Armeda Snow Young, and their eight children. And he was living his dream as an actor, singer, cross-dresser, and church leader. He had it all! But God came first, so Morris worked for the LDS Church like his dad, Brigham Young, wanted.

CHAPTER 22
THE TRAIN LEAVES AT MIDNIGHT

A soft summer breeze was blowing. The streets were empty, with no carriages, riders, or passersby. Two women were walking at a fast pace down Price Street, headed for the Salt Lake train station. It was 11:35 p.m. Across the street, scurrying in the same direction, was a tall, sturdy gentleman with wavy dirty-blonde hair. His objective was blood atonement; he'd been sent by the Prophet.

Earlier That Evening

Three letters written on white linen paper were addressed to the Prophet Brigham Young and left on his desk.

The first letter read as follows:
Dear Husband,

It is with deep regret that I must leave you and the children. My heart is heavy with sorrow and despair. While my religious views haven't changed, the oppression that you have placed upon my heart is too much to bear. You have not been in my bed for four years, which makes me feel ugly, unattractive, and fat. Everyone says I am not fat, just pleasingly plump with large breasts and short in stature. Praying diligently every night for your pleasurable touch did not work. It appears God has turned a deaf ear. A man could get a divorce if his wife were to withhold sexual favors. Your theocratic leadership has done me in, so to speak. Also, you always said if we left you, our children must remain in your care. They are sleeping now. Please comfort them when they awake. My dear sweet children will need their father more than ever now that their mother has fled.

Gertrude Ann
The second letter read as follows:
Dear Prophet,

You had known me since I was fourteen when my life became bittersweet. You hurt me that first night. I cried out, but you kept on thrusting my womanhood. I couldn't sit for a week. Nine months later, Jeremy and Jacob were born—the joys of my present mediocre existence. The boys are now twelve—the age of reason to join the Aaronic priesthood. Our daughters, Cynthia, Rachel, and Mary, are sleeping like angels. They are strong like you and will make fine wives someday. They know how to bake huge cinnamon buns and yeast rolls that measure five inches tall—the way to a Mormon husband's heart.

I have missed your presence in my bed for the last five years. O, how I have desired one more thrust. The sad thing is that you will never miss me. Only our children will do that. Please make sure Rachel drinks her Mormon tea daily to avoid an asthma attack.

Stay well, my Prophet,
Mary Katherine
The third letter read as follows:
Brigham,

I will return in a month. This short time should give Clarence enough time to find a suitable house to live in. He will no longer be an embarrassment for you, my darling, running through the streets of Salt Lake in young girl's attire—dresses, wigs, hats, lace-up boots—with red rouge and lipstick on his face. You must admit he makes a pretty sight. His baritone voice and musical talents shall not go to waste in California. He will be able to be himself and reach artistic heights. I will wire you my return date. Please do not be angry; it will all work out for the better. The train leaves at midnight; I must hurry.

Love and friendship,
Margaret Joyce

At the train station, the gentleman who'd been following the two women stood tall on the wooden platform, watching them board the train. Then he noticed Clarence sitting with his mother in their compartment. Shortly thereafter, he saw Gertrude Ann and Mary Katherine sit down across from them. He thought about being a fly on the wall, listening to their conversation about their life with Brigham, which could fill a twenty-chapter book. He also thought about the days of his youth when these women fed him chocolate chip cookies, ham salad sandwiches, turkey dinners with all the fixings, and his annual German chocolate birthday cake with tiny blue homemade candles. And, oh yes, those delicious biscuits and spicy sausage gravy, rare roast beef and brown mushroom gravy over buttered mashed potatoes, and baked apple strudel with vanilla ice cream. *It is hard to kill these women who doted on me like real mothers and fed me so well. I love these women still. There will be hell to pay in the morning when I meet with the Prophet. I am not afraid to have my throat cut. These women deserve a second chance at happiness.*

Brigham's Office the Next Morning

As John D. Lee fell to his knees, tears ran down his bruised and swollen cheeks.

"Father, I couldn't kill them. Please forgive me, but they raised me. All I could think of was all the love and food they gave me so generously. Perhaps they will return to you one day and feel remorseful." John D. Lee bowed his head and started to sob.

"You have disappointed me for the first time, Son, but I understand your reluctance. Mary Katherine's cherry pie was irresistible, with fresh whipped cream on top. I will miss her baking skills. Nevertheless, her relationship with Gertrude Ann is unholy, and they will never get into celestial heaven. I refuse to knock on their doors. Let me pray about what my responsibility is. The Lord will guide me. Perhaps I will have a change of heart regarding their fate. I'm only human. How much can I take when my wives decide to leave me? I do have feelings even though I am the strongest and toughest man in Utah Territory. But for now, Son, I need you to return to your ferry post in Arizona. Let's pray for your safe return.

"Heavenly Father, thank you for all the blessings you have bestowed upon me and my people. Please guide my son John home safely, as he is a good boy with sincere intentions, even though he messed up his assignment. But maybe it was your will. Also, Lord, please grant me guidance to preserve the principle in other lands outside Utah Territory. The federal government is attempting to eradicate plural marriage all over the United States, even here in Zion, so I will need your help, Father, to save us. Amen!"

After John left, the prophet knelt and prayed for forgiveness for not carrying out the blood atonement ritual that was necessary for these two wives, who were great bakers, to reach celestial heaven.

"I am at a loss, Father. Please guide my thoughts and deeds. I shall put the matter to rest until I receive your guidance. Amen!" Brigham prayed.

Back on the Train

"Well, we did it, ladies; we escaped polygamy and the wrath of the Prophet," said Gertrude Ann.

"We left letters on his desk saying our goodbyes," added Mary Katherine.

"I did the same," said Margaret. "My note was short and to the point. It has been twenty-five years since Brigham and I married; he didn't even remember our anniversary this year, which was the last blow. I gave him six sons and three daughters; all their births were difficult. My second baby was breech, and I thought I was going to die. But I want much more for Clarence; he deserves to live a full life, one he chooses, not a profession his father desires, which will certainly stifle his creativity and musical talents," Margaret said.

"You know, you are in big trouble taking his son away from him. He will never forgive you. He will hunt you and young Clarence down until his avenging angels find him. We left our children with their nanny, Angela," Mary Katherine added.

"But my note specifically said I would return in one month—but without Clarence. Brigham gets embarrassed by his cross-dressing," Margaret said.

"Why return at all?" Gertrude Ann asked.

Margaret smiled and said with confidence, "I am going to inherit a fortune when my husband passes on. It is rumored that Brigham is a multimillionaire and will leave just his remaining wives an equal share of his money and possessions."

"Gee, maybe we should have stayed, Gertrude Ann?" Mary Katherine asked.

"No way! You can't put a price on freedom," Gertrude Ann answered.

All three women and Clarence agreed on that last point. Soon they decided it was time to retire to their private berths, singing, "God is great, God is good, God believes in freedom!"

CHAPTER 23
WRANGLERS AND RUSTLERS ON THE ARIZONA STRIP

The Arizona Strip was filled with mystery and intrigue. It was situated in the northern part of Arizona and bordered on the west by California and Nevada, on the east by New Mexico Territory, on the north by Utah Territory, and on the south by the Colorado River and Mexico. Originally owned by Mexico, this strip became part of the United States after the war between Mexico and the United States in 1836. It was barren land until ditches were dug, allowing water to flow down from mountain streams to the corn and wheat crops. This barren land became fertile and offered great potential for agriculture, making it ripe for a Mormon settlement. The first Mormon explorer to visit the strip was Jacob Hamblin in the mid-1850s. Then in the 1870s, Brigham Young commissioned some of his trusted friends to settle this strip of land. His purpose was to spread the principle of plural marriage. He knew the only way Utah Territory could become a state of the Union was to end polygamy, which it did on April 4, 1890. So, prior to that date, many plural marriages occurred that tripled the number of children who were born into the LDS Church. The Prophet had had great foresight and vision, which paid off.

Between 1870 and 1890, many wonderful events occurred on the Arizona Strip. Better dams were constructed with iron and wood piers, which kept water in place. Originally eleven dams were built to store domestic and agricultural water, but these were destroyed a few days after the annual spring thaw. The first settlement was called Littlefield, which was situated on the west side of the strip. It was close to St. George, where a beautiful Mormon temple was built. John Bushman and Thomas Huntzmon, along with William Allen and John D. Lee, were sent to the middle and eastern part of the strip where the Little Colorado River snaked around the canyons and valleys. Since every Mormon was there for the same purpose, and because the water was key to their success, they all worked together to settle and colonize this magnificent land with purple sage for God and country.

Soon many ranches sprouted up, and LDS chapels were built. On any given night, the Mormon settlers could be visited by rustlers from the south and east who would steal the cookies from the outdoor bins that were conveniently placed on the front porch for the children, so they could snack on the cookies while they were doing their chores. These thieves loved Mormon baked goods. If they came to steal horses at night, they would take all the pies that were cooling on the porches. They showed no mercy; they didn't even leave one for breakfast. Just plain greedy pigs!

One summer evening in June, Thomas was wrangling with the Udalls on their five-hundred-acre ranch southeast of Joseph City. He was helping them gather the mother cows and their calves to wrangle to a greener pasture that had branding chutes. The deep velvet pasture looked so inviting and smelled so sweet that the calves never knew they were going to be branded. It was summertime. They just frolicked in the sun before it vanished at 8:51 p.m., nursed on their mothers' teats, and played with other calves.

Then one day, all hell broke loose; the babies were separated from their mothers. Hired hands were in short supply this year, so the Arizona ranchers formed their own posse to help each other out with this labor-intensive but important chore. The pasture was noisy, with cries from the young calves. It was bittersweet to help as these cute little babies were burnt with the brand for ten seconds. Their screams made the blood curdle as if it was your first-time branding. Smoke was puffing from the chutes, and it smelled like a barbecue on a Sunday afternoon. The chutes were made of wood—from the nearby ash trees in the mountains—and thrown together without nails. It was the careful way the logs were put together that made the chutes sturdy and straight. Sometimes the calves got lucky if there was a pond nearby; they could walk over to it and cover their new brands with cool water. Nevertheless, branding stung the calves for a bit but eventually subsided. And the little critters grew up to become great roasts and chicken-fried steaks for Sunday dinner.

"Mr. Udall, would you be willing to sell me some calves? I plan on starting my spread now that my family will be joining me soon," Thomas said.

Udall smiled and said, "Of course. You've been a big help to me, always ready to help when I needed extra hands to round up my herd. How many, Thomas?"

Thomas gladly responded, "About fifty heifers and one bull."

"Well, I will throw in one more bull for good measure and only charge you forty dollars apiece for the heifers," Mr. Udall said.

"Yippee!" Thomas shouted. Forty dollars sounded perfect and fit his tithing budget. He thought the price sounded fair for the choice of Black Baldy Herefords, so he responded with a yes. The two men shook hands, and the deal was sealed. Thomas now had something to start his Arizona ranch with to increase his investment, but he needed one more thing, a grand two-story brick ranch home with white turrets, porches, and a flat roof surrounded by a strong white picket fence to have parties on, plus a basement where Katryn could can and store food, along with water, for a year. *I will probably build this home in Snowflake—named after apostle Erastus Snow and the Mormon land agent William Jordon Flake,* he thought. *It will only be a few miles from the Huntzmon ranch; plus, it's a short, easy ride from town.*

Katryn and the family will love their new home, Thomas pondered. *It's so big; everyone will have lots of closet space and their own room. There will be four Jack and Jill bathrooms and a master suite with its own bathtub and two large thunder pots. The kitchen will have two stoves—one for baking and one for cooking—and an eight-foot-tall, five-foot-wide mahogany dish cabinet with beveled glass doors. There will also be three white porcelain sinks—one for soaking, one for washing, and one for standing. The living room will be formal with two green velvet couches and four Queen Anne chairs. In the middle of the open family area, there will be located, in front of the fireplace, a baby grand piano for Katryn to teach piano lessons to our children and play church hymns on family night. She is very musically astute, which is one of the reasons I love her so much. Plus, she promised to teach me to play some Christmas carols such as "Silent Night" and "Away in a Manger." Well, it's getting late, and I must pen my darling Katryn a love letter.*

CHAPTER 24
TWO LETTERS

My Dearest Katryn,

I hope this letter finds you and the children doing well. I miss you, my sweet darling. It is sad to sleep at night without your warm body next to mine. I am staying with Brother Bushman, who is in the process of building his big home in St. Joseph. He has taken a second wife, while his first wife, Lois, is in Orem with their children. Eventually, Lois and the kids will join her husband in Arizona. At that time, I will have to find another place to camp further east, a few miles from the dam I am working on. I am roughing it for now, saving our pesos for our big home with all the amenities.

Katryn, at first, there were four Mormon settlements in northern Arizona, but now there is only St. Joseph—named after our first Prophet, Joseph Smith. Life here in the desert is difficult without enough irrigation water to grow crops and with dams that continually fall apart. Water is to ranchers like gold is to miners—very precious. We desperately need water for our livestock and human consumption. But there is a new rare breed of hardy cattle down here; they can survive on the brush and can go without water longer than any other breeds. They are called Texas Longhorns. Originally from Spain, they were shipped to the West Indies and then were moved on to Mexico and Texas. Honey, their horns can be up to ten feet wide—and both bulls and cows have them.

They are something to watch when they mate. Their calves are very friendly since they get lots of love from their mamas. We can make lots of money from selling these cattle. I shall bring a bull home to mate with our heifers and make them stronger. The desert is a playground for them, as it is for our Herefords, which need plenty of water to prosper in the desert around the ranch. I truly believe a cross between these two breeds will pay off at the bank, my darling.

Katryn, the new dam is progressing slowly; once we think it's fixed and ready to go, it falls apart. I spent many hours figuring it out, and I finally discovered the secret. The dam must be ten feet wide on the bottom and fifteen feet wide on top and will serve lateral ditches leading to the farmers' crops. The dam has been fortified with stronger wood and metal piles and thicker brush. That's how they hold up dams in the Netherlands. One of our missionaries who did his mission there brought us their secret. We are also going to use larger, heavier boulders that will not roll away. All this will take more time and will keep me from seeing you, darling, in a few weeks, but I will work diligently to kiss and hug you soon. I promise! Just three more weeks, then I will return to you, honey. Mark off your calendar for two weeks just for us; we've got a lot of catching up to do.

Afterward, we will pack only the essentials to survive in this wilderness, then head south with our family. There we will build our new brick home in Snowflake by the Cottonwood and Silver Creeks. Honey, the bricks now come by train, premade in Wisconsin. The train will bring more Mormons here as it did for Utah. It is a lot faster than covered wagons and handcarts. Our ancestors really suffered during those long trail rides and walk from the East to the West until they reached Salt Lake City.

Katryn, you are going to love it down here. The Arizona Strip is beautiful in the springtime with all the flowering cacti—red, yellow, and fuchsia. And the huge white sego lilies are shaped like trumpets with long necks and round mouths with golden tongues. We will ride into the Arizona sunset, which is unbelievable around eight, with its deep purple and pinkish clouds offset with a bright orange burst of sunshine. Then we can take a ride down to Cottonwood Creek and take a moonlight swim and make mad, passionate love.

Brigham still wants us to move here and colonize the church. He is still asking me to take a second wife, but I have refused. It's just you and me, darling, forever and ever. Honey, please stay safe until you are in my arms once again. I will see you in my dreams. God bless you!

Thomas

Katryn read Thomas's letter, and tears streamed down her sullen face. *Oh, darling,* she thought, *I miss you so much. My stomach aches when I feel for your warm face on our big brass bed. Your sweet smile and tender touch are missing. Darling, when you return, I am planning to make all your favorite meals with no complaints about the corned beef and cabbage smell. And our bedroom looks different; I have made new blue curtains with a matching bedspread and four pillow shams. You're going to love the new pillow top I made for our king-size bed. The doctor said it would help your back pain from horseback riding and being bucked off our prize bull, Matches. Come the first Sunday you are home, and we will invite all the neighbors to a barbecue with all the fixings: pork and beef ribs, baked beans with onions and bacon strips, and potato salad with dill, sour cream, and hard-boiled eggs. We'll also have cornbread, sweet butter, and honey by the bucketful, along with freshly squeezed cold apple cider and a big chocolate cake with whipped cream icing.*

As Katryn looked out her sunny bedroom window, she couldn't imagine finding another place like this ranch. But she knew she must follow her church and her husband's wishes and relocate to the Arizona Strip. Perhaps she could appoint someone else to work the Underground Railroad. Yes, Thomas's mother and sister said they would help, and they had met John Gaynor, who would be glad to help them. Besides, they didn't follow polygamy; not every Mormon family did. *Yes! Esther and Sarah will be perfect for carrying with my work. They hate polygamy!*

Three weeks seemed like two months to Katryn. Time stood still before her husband would be home. But she made the best of the time to prepare for his coming. Then Katryn changed her mind about moving after reading the *Salt Lake Tribune*. Brigham Young had died from appendicitis. She was hoping the new church Prophet, Wilford Woodruff, would not want Thomas in Arizona. Her cheeks turned pink, and her heart skipped a beat. She was happy once again with the hope of a life in the place that she and Thomas now called home. Before retiring to bed, Katryn penned a letter to Thomas.

A Letter from Katryn

My Dearest Thomas,

You are my hero, my mentor, and my life. Without you, I am incomplete. Your touch is electrifying; your kiss boils my blood; your eyes pierce my soul; your courage excites me; your love haunts me; and your absence has been intolerable. I pray for the moment we entwine like vines, my sweet darling, hoping our union is soon.

Your letter was a breath of fresh air. You are in a bold new world of dangerous

surprises: rustlers killing sheep; stealing water and cattle; burning ranches; raping and murdering Mormons; and crippling mares to harvest their foals. Brigham told me last week at Conference before he died that you were doing a great job for the church. He was very proud of you, my husband. He also said the sacrifices we have made by being apart would be rewarded in celestial heaven, where our exaltation will be greater than gold.

All I want is to see your handsome tanned face with that charming cowboy smile. Your life sounds dangerous in Arizona. I'm not sure the children and I should join you in St. Joseph yet. They have a healthy, sunny, prosperous life here on the ranch. The Palace Hotel is still buying our cattle, which are still being shipped by rail from Salt Lake. We are very rich, my darling. Perhaps it is time you came home and just increased your tithe to send someone else to replace you. Your strength and wisdom are needed here at home. I know you are not a coward, Thomas, but your family needs you *too*!

Love always,
Katryn

CHAPTER 25
A NEAR-DEATH EXPERIENCE

"I'm coming around the mountain, yes I am. I'm going to John Lee's Ferry, yes, I am. On my way home to Katryn, going to see my seven children. I'll have supper with them tomorrow; yes, I will."

Suddenly the singing stopped. Thomas felt a sharp, piercing pain in his right shoulder. It felt like there was a burning arrow plunging through it. There was blood running down his shirt sleeve. He heard his heart pound faster. Sweat began pouring down his cheeks. His vision was failing. The horizon was far off in the foggy distance. As Thomas's crippled body fell on top of Brave Eagle's silky mane, he knew he was in serious trouble. Practically blind in both eyes from the pain, he managed to turn his horse in the direction of Lee's Ferry. There, he knew, he would get nursing assistance from John Lee's wife, Agnes, the best nurse in northern Arizona and Utah Territory.

After a week of high fever and chills, Thomas's fever broke. He opened his eyes and yelled Katryn's name. He saw her blue eyes and inviting smile, then passed out.

When he awoke the next morning, he saw Mrs. Lee wiping his forehead with a cold rag. He recognized her.

"Mrs. Lee, where is my Katryn? I saw her here. Her blue eyes were looking straight into mine. Please, where is she? Katryn? Katryn?" he yelled, but he passed out again.

When Thomas opened his eyes a third time, he saw those pretty blue eyes staring at him again.

"Good morning, Mr. Thomas. I am Celinda, Mrs. Lee's assistant nurse."

"What happened to me, and where is my horse?"

"Your horse is getting fat—needs someone to ride him. As for you, you were near death. A poison arrow hit the back of your left shoulder and did damage to your muscles. You will need to rest that arm in this cotton sleeve. Also, I will apply a poultice made from healing herbs—a mixture of turmeric and sage—on your wound four times a day when I change your bandages. It will extract the poison and pain from where the arrow entered. By the way, Thomas, it was an Apache who got you. One killed my husband last spring. They're nasty people sometimes. Never heard a good word said about them."

"You speak mighty fine English for a squaw. Your eyes are baby blue, just like those of my wife, Katryn. But she is paler and taller, and her hair is the color of gold with reddish streaks. When I first opened my eyes and saw your baby blues, I said her name, thinking you were her. I hope I didn't offend you much. I couldn't see well. But now my vision is perfect. And I can smell it too. Like those biscuits and gravy coming from the kitchen. May I have some, please?" Thomas asked.

"You may have all you want. A hearty breakfast will surely help with healing. I'll throw in some scrambled eggs with cheese. A wound like yours needs lots of protein. The Lees raise their own pigs and make a tasty breakfast pork steak with hot spices; that will also help you get better faster. And I'm not bragging, but I make the best apricot juice to wash down all that delicious food."

As Celinda gathered breakfast, Thomas couldn't help but notice her small, sensuous shape, her long shiny black hair pulled back in a French braid, and those piercing blue eyes. He thought her to be attractive but not as beautiful as his Katryn and well-educated in nursing. Her English was perfect. If he closed his eyes when Celinda spoke, he would see her as white in his mind.

Breakfast came, and not another sound did Thomas utter except "Amen." He purposely shortened grace from three sentences to just one word.

He chowed down like a regular cowhand, but he was having trouble eating with only his right hand. He couldn't cut anything.

"Darn, Celinda, I am becoming very frustrated. Would you please help a wounded man by cutting his pork steak into small pieces, please? I am so famished, I just want to gobble everything up with my hand, but that would not be eating like the gentleman I was raised to be," Thomas proclaimed.

"I would be happy to help you, Thomas. I know just how difficult it can be to eat with only one hand. I have broken my wrist once and my shoulder twice—one on each side."

"How about telling me a story about your life? I find you very interesting, Celinda."

"Okay, but you'll think I have lived a sheltered life."
"Let me be the judge of that," Thomas replied.

"I am Ute and Spanish," she said softly. "My great-grandfather Don De La Vega was a conquistador searching for gold. Eventually, he returned Spain a very wealthy man, but he left his progeny, my grandfather, here since he would not be welcomed by his family in Spain because polygamy was a foreign practice in Europe. Only Muslims had more than one wife. Some Jews used to practice plural marriage in ancient times, but not in the nineteenth century."

"You sure are smart. Plus, I can't get over your Native Mexican accent; it sounds American." Thomas chuckled with excitement. "Did you go to formal school?"

"Of course, I did. I attended the Sisters of Loretto Catholic School for Girls [Academy of Our Lady of Light] in Santa Fe," Celinda answered with her nose in the air and a big smile on her face, "and I plan to attend Dartmouth to study medicine in the fall. Then I'll return to the reservation after graduation and help my people stay healthy. I will also set up a school for midwives and surgical nurses to assist me in breech births."

After breakfast, the young Navajo widow changed Thomas's bandage after first putting on a strong herbal poultice of berry root, aloe, and turmeric to draw out the infection. Then Celinda applied a fresh cold rag to Thomas's forehead to keep his fever down. The arrow that had shot him was dipped in snake venom, which kills quickly. Thomas was lucky John D. had given him a blessing by rubbing blessed oil on his head. That act, along with the application of the poultices, saved his life. The arrow was destined for his heart. It also could be said in Mormon thought that the holy church garments gave some protection, as prophesied by Joseph Smith from his dream of seeing garments on the angel Moroni. Nevertheless, it took two weeks for Thomas to heal and get back on his feet. He said his goodbyes and triple-thanked everyone for helping him get better, especially Celinda.

"I will miss my sweet nurse who gives great neck massages. Celinda, may I ask you a personal question? Have you ever thought of marrying again?" Thomas asked in a very soft, self-assured voice.

Celinda smiled and shrugged her shoulders. She responded, "Maybe, if the right one comes along." She did feel her heart flutter, though, looking at his handsome physique as he sat tall in his saddle with his piercing blue eyes and gargantuan smile. His lips were very pink and kissable, she thought. But he would never fit in with her culture. And she didn't believe in polygamy.

Thomas hugged her and kissed her on her forehead, thinking to himself how lucky he was to have had Celinda's help. He wouldn't have made it without her expert nursing skills, for he'd been near death. He rode off into the Arizona sunset, thanking God all the way back to his ranch for his good fortune.

A month after Katryn mailed her letter, she received a telegram from Thomas. It only had twenty-one words:

PLEASE MEET ME IN SALT LAKE. STOP.
MOTHER'S DAY. STOP.
COME WITH THE CHILDREN. STOP.

THERE IS SOMEONE SPECIAL I WANT YOU TO MEET. STOP.

Oh dear, Katryn thought, then she passed out on the bed. When she awoke, she gathered the children and discussed the trip back to see their father in Salt Lake. They were all looking forward to seeing him on Mother's Day, which was only one week away. As Katryn passed the guest room, she wondered who would be living there. *I just refuse to believe that Thomas has taken another wife without consulting with me. He truly loves only me, and he wouldn't dare! He kept his word and vows never to take another wife. Besides, Thomas knows I would leave him and take the children back to New York, where the boys would dress up in silly clothes, which he abhors, and the girls would attend college and become career women first before marrying. And we would join the Presbyterian Church and not wear our church garments. Only God can get us out of this mess. Thomas wouldn't put us through this turmoil; he just wouldn't,* she thought. Katryn continued to rest on her marriage bed, looking out the window onto a warm spring evening. The golden moon was full, and the stars were shining like a thousand tiny diamonds. Katryn closed her eyes and fell into a deep sleep, dreaming of her sweetheart.

To be continued in the Quilt of Many Colors Vol II

APPENDIX: TIMELINE OF THE CHURCH OF LATTER-DAY SAINTS, 1805–1846—NEW YORK TO UTAH TERRITORY, THE NORTHERN ARIZONA STRIP, AND MEXICO

Timeline of the Church of Latter-day Saints, 1805–1846—New York to Utah Territory, the Northern Arizona Strip, and Mexico

1805—Joseph Smith is born.

1820—God the Father and His Son Jesus Christ appeared to Joseph Smith.

1823—The angel Moroni first appears to Joseph Smith.

1827—Joseph Smith receives the golden plates.

1829—Joseph Smith completes the translation of the Book of Mormon.

1829—The Aaronic and Melchizedek priesthoods are restored.

1830—The Book of Mormon is published in Palmyra, New York.

1830—The church is organized.

1831—The Lord designates Independence, Missouri, as the city of Zion.

1832—Brigham Young is baptized into the LDS Church.

1833—The saints in Jackson County, Missouri, are forced to leave the county.

1833—Word of Wisdom is established: drinking alcohol or smoking are not permitted, and the eating of proper foods is encouraged.

1834—Joseph Smith and other church leaders move to Far West, Missouri.

1835—The Quorum of the Twelve Apostles and the First Quorum of the Seventy are organized.

1836—The Kirtland Temple is dedicated.

1836—Priesthood keys are committed to Joseph Smith and Oliver Cowdery in the Kirtland Temple.

1838—Joseph Smith and other church leaders move to Far West, Missouri.

1839—Joseph Smith joins the saints in Illinois and helps establish Nauvoo.

1842—The Relief Society is organized.

1843—Revelation on eternal marriage and plural wives (D&C 132) is recorded.

1844—Joseph and Hyrum Smith are assassinated.

1844—The Quorum of the Twelve Apostles is sustained to lead the church.

1846—Many saints begin their journey to the Salt Lake Valley.

1846 The Nauvoo Temple is dedicated.

1846—Brigham Young becomes the prophet and president of the LDS Church and leads the Mormon migration westward.

1847—Brigham Young enters the Great Salt Lake Valley.

1847–67—More than seventy pioneers settle in Utah.

1848—Brigham Young reveals the location of the future Salt Lake Temple.

1849—Brigham Young organizes the provisional state of Deseret.

1850—Deseret becomes the Utah Territory.

1850—A board of regents organized by Brigham Young established the University of Deseret, which later became the University of Utah.

1851—United States president Milliard Fillmore appointed Brigham Young first territorial governor of the Utah Territory.

1853—Brigham Young breaks ground for the construction of the new temple.

1857—Meadows Mountain Massacre occurs approximately thirty miles from Cedar City.

1877—Brigham Young presides at the dedication of St. George Temple.

1877—Brigham Young dies at the age of seventy-six from a ruptured appendix.

GLOSSARY OF MORMON TERMS

This glossary aims to help readers of The Quilt of Many Colors understand this story through the point of view of a Mormon in the nineteenth century.

Aaronic priesthood. Holders are twelve to eighteen years of age and perform specific duties in the Church of Latter-day Saints (such as preparing, blessing, and administering the sacrament, and possibly performing some baptisms).

Avenging Angels, Danites. A fraternal organization founded by Latter-day Saints members in June 1838 in Missouri. Their chief purpose was to protect LDS leaders and their church.

Blood atonement. A Mormon belief that the death of Jesus did not wash away heinous crimes; the only way for sinners of this description to enter celestial heaven was to slit their own throats—or one of the Danites would do it.

Book of Mormon. A history of the ancestors of Mormons who traveled to North America from Israel—Nephites, Laminites, and the Jaredites.

Gentile. A religious term the Mormons use to speak about anyone who is not a Mormon.

Handcart. The Mormon pioneers who couldn't afford a wagon used a handcart made of wood with two big wheels and round wooden arms to transport their belongings. This practice began in 1856.

Haun's Mill Massacre. On October 30, 1838, a Mormon settlement in eastern Caldwell County, Missouri, was attacked by a mob from Livingston County, Missouri. This mob consisted of 240

Missouri Regulators, state militiamen, and anti-Mormon volunteers. There were seventeen deaths, and fifteen Mormons were injured.

Melchizedek priesthood. The power and authority of God are conferred upon worthy members of the Church of Jesus Christ of Latter-day Saints.

Mormon dogma. The core teachings of the Church of Latter-day Saints.

Mormonism. An American-made religion started by Joseph Smith. The Mormons' main belief about God is that he is a man, and any man can reach the status of God, but no one has.

Mountain Meadows Massacre. On October 11, 1857, the Fancher party from Arkansas was attacked by Paiute, Mormons dressed as Native Americans, and the Mormon Battalion, and 120 innocent pioneers—men, women, and children over the age of seven—were massacred. There were seventeen survivors, all children under the age of eight.

Polygamy. The marriage of one man to more than one woman simultaneously is practiced by some Mormons with the purpose of producing many children to proselytize the Mormon dogma.

Principle, the. Refers to the sanctity of plural marriage found in polygamy.

Smith, Joseph. The first leader and president of the Church of Jesus Christ of Latter-day Saints, he was martyred on June 27, 1844.

Transportation modes the Mormons used.
Mormon Trail. The thirteen-hundred-mile route that members of the Church of Jesus Christ of Latter-day Saints traveled from 1846 to 1868. Its location was in Illinois, Iowa, Nebraska, Wyoming, and Utah.

Transcontinental Railway (Union Pacific). A 1,912-mile continuous railroad line constructed between 1863 and 1869, connecting the existing eastern US rail network at Omaha, Nebraska/ Council

Bluffs, Iowa, with the Pacific Coast at the Oakland Long Wharf on San Francisco Bay.

Western Underground Railway (the Freedom Trail—before 1869).

Word of Wisdom. A health code used by the Church of Latter-day Saints forbids the use of coffee, tea, and alcoholic beverages; advises use of less meat; and promotes eating more fruits, vegetables, and grains.

Young, Brigham. The greatest leader of the Mormon Church, who led the Mormons to Utah Territory. He was the second president of the Church of Latter-day Saints. He died on August 29, 1877.

ZCMI. Zion's Cooperative Mercantile Institution, the first department store in the United States, was founded by Brigham Young in 1868 and is presently owned by Macy's and Dillard's. It had over one hundred retail outlets in Utah during the 1800s.

NOTES

The Quilt of Many Colors, representing the LDS Church and its members from a variety of nationalities around the world, is a fictional love story woven into nineteenth-century US history. Nothing written herein should be perceived as true but as a figment of my vivid imagination.

SUGGESTED READING

The following are resources that have had the greatest effect on my writing of this novel. Please feel free to read them and discover the wealth of US history that I discovered while doing my research. I wove details from the early days of New York City in the 1600s, including the influences of the mighty Dutch, the French and Indian War, the decadent and cruel reign of England over the thirteen original colonies, the Westward Expansion of the United States, the Civil War, the building of the Transcontinental Railroad and the Union Pacific, with the political and religious influences that shaped the West.

Brooks, Juanita. *Mt. Meadows Massacre*. Oklahoma City: University of Oklahoma Press, 1962.

Burrows, Edwin G., and Mike Wallace. *Gotham: A History of New York City to 1898*. New York, Oxford: Oxford University Press, 1943.

Bushman, Vaughn. *From Edelweiss to Sego Lily*. Scottsdale, AZ: Wilshire Press, 2009.

Carmack, John Kay. *Astride History: Nauvoo to Utah to Arizona*. With John Bushman. Salt Lake City: Church of Jesus Christ of Latter-day Saints Printing Division, 2014.

Ebershoff, David. *The 19th Wife*. New York: Random House, 2009.

Grey, Zane. *Desert Heritage: A Western Story*. Thorndike Press, 2010.

———. *Riders of the Purple Sage*. New York: Tom Doherty Associates, 2014. First published in 1912.

———. *Union Pacific: A Western Story*. Five Star, 1918.

———. *Woman of the Frontier.* Five Star, 1998.

Krakauer, Jon. *Under the Banner of Heaven.* New York: Anchor Books, 2004.

Landon, Michael N., and Brandon Metcalf Jr. *History of the Saints: The Remarkable Journey of the Mormon Battalion.* American Fork, UT: Covenant Communications, 2012.

Miller, Rod. *Father unto Many Sons.* Five Star, 2018.

Newell, Linda King. *Emma Hale Smith: Mormon Enigma.* Urbana: University of Illinois Press, 1994.

Stenhouse, Fanny, and Harriet Beecher Stowe. *Tell It All: A Woman's Life in Polygamy.* Whitefish, MT: Kessinger Legacy Reprints, Kessinger Publishing, 2010. First published in 1874.

The Teachings of Presidents of the Church: Joseph Smith. Salt Lake City: Intellectual Reserve, 2007.

Wallace, Mike. *Greater Gotham: A History of New York City from 1898 to 1919.* Oxford, England: Oxford University Press, 2017.

Ingram Content Group UK Ltd.
Milton Keynes UK
UKHW020844130423
420096UK00007B/53